The
William HILL
Book of
RACING
QUOTATIONS
Graham Sharpe

GW00696816

STANLEY PAUL

First published 1994

1 3 5 7 9 10 8 6 4 2

Copyright © Graham Sharpe 1994

Graham Sharpe has asserted his right under the
Copyright, Designs and Patents Act 1988 to be identified
as the author of this work

First published in the United Kingdom in 1994
by Stanley Paul & Co. Ltd
Random House, 20 Vauxhall Bridge Road
London SW1V 2SA

Random House Australia (Pty) Limited
20 Alfred Street, Milsons Point, Sydney
New South Wales 2061, Australia

Random House New Zealand Limited
19 Poland Road, Glenfield
Auckland 10, New Zealand

Random House South Africa (Pty) Limited
PO Box 337, Bergvlei, South Africa

Random House UK Limited Reg. No. 954009

A CIP catalogue record for this book is available
from the British Library

ISBN 0 09 179084 0

Design & make up Roger Walker/Graham Harmer

Printed and bound in Great Britain by
Clays Ltd, St Ives plc

PHOTOGRAPH ACKNOWLEDGEMENTS

The author and publisher would like to thank Colorsport and
George Selwyn for allowing the use of copyright photographs as
follows:

Colorsport: pages 10, 26, 47, 79, 123, 138, 158.
George Selwyn: pages 5, 17, 19, 30, 44, 50, 57, 61, 66, 76, 85, 89,
95, 102, 106, 129, 133, 142, 145, 147, 154/5, 160, 168.

CONTENTS

INTRODUCTION

Compiling a book of this kind bestows an unexpected feeling of power in that it might be possible to make or break a reputation by judicious, or injudicious manipulation of a quote. For example, if I were a critic of Lester Piggott and the Derby winner Sir Ivor, I might choose to include a comment by a respected racing journalist, Roger Mortimer, from a piece of his about the 1968 Epsom triumph – 'No wonder horse'. This might imply a lack of respect for the combination on the part of Mr Mortimer. However, this would be less than accurate, as the full quote is, in fact: 'No wonder horse and rider were cheered to the echo as they entered the winner's enclosure'.

So, there is great responsibility not to take quotations too much out of context, and I hope I have not done that. I also happen to have what some have described as a rather perverse sense of humour so, if the relevance of a particularly pithy extract eludes you, I'm sure this is more likely to be a failing of mine than yours – I don't think! Nor do I make any apologies for appending the odd personal comment, aside or criticism to some of the quotations. I know it might be regarded as cowardly to answer back to someone who can't have the last word, but as the excerpts and extracts were dug out and selected by me I reserve the right to let you know just what I think of them. If you don't approve, then just ignore them – or, better still, write your own comments about my comments in the margin.

On a more serious note, although entirely self-contained, this book is intended as a companion volume to 1988's *Book Of Racing Quotations*, also from the Stanley Paul stable, and compiled by Nick Robinson and David Llewellyn. Thus I have concentrated on up-dating the concept by including a majority of contemporary material dating from late 1988 up until mid-1994. But when I have come across classic comments from down the years which did not figure in that earlier book I have included them.

As ever, a book of this nature must by definition draw from a vast variety of sources, both verbal and printed – books, interviews, newspapers, magazines, etc, have been ransacked in the search for the pithy, scurrilous, unguarded, insightful, rude, humorous, thoughtful or just plain interesting. Wherever possible and appropriate, permission to reproduce has been sought – so, advance apologies to anyone who feels they have been overlooked.

Finally, thanks are due to my employers, bookmakers William Hill, for supporting this venture and, of course, to all at Stanley Paul – in particular, my Editor, Marion Paull for making it possible and for being sympathetic about my choice of football teams to support – Luton Town and Wealdstone FC.

Graham Sharpe

THE LADIES

The wrong shape

Their bottoms are the wrong shape.

LESTER PIGGOTT's opinion of female jockeys, recorded in the *Guinness Book of Great Jockeys of the Flat* Guinness, 1992

I still don't approve of women jockeys – except in point-to-points and hunter chases, of course. Really, they're not the right make or shape for it.

Trainer MERCY RIMELL in *Reflections of Racing* Pelham Books, 1990

The chances of me or any other successful lady jockey getting into the big league is nil.

ALEX 'Queen of the Sand' GREAVES, who made her name on the all-weather surface at Southwell, reported in the *Guinness Book of Great Jockeys of the Flat* Guinness, 1992

Women jockeys are a pain. Jumping's a man's game. They are not built like us. Most of them are as strong as half a Disprin.

STEVE SMITH-ECCLES, asked for his thoughts on Gee Armytage's chances in the 1988 Grand National

I don't think National Hunt is a game for women. At the end of a three-mile chase . . . women are just not strong enough.

Record-breaking woman point-to-point rider ALISON DARE *The Times* 14 January 1994

She lost over 84lb and she weighs in now at 98lb.

BETTY McTAGUE, mother of recently arrived on the scene Canadian jockey Miriam 'Mini' McTague who, presumably, knows all about riding a 'weighting' race having lost virtually half of her body weight to take up the career *Racing Post* 13 May 1994

There are some owners and trainers who simply will not put up a woman jockey, no matter how capable she may be.

GEE ARMYTAGE in *Gee – The Diary of a National Hunt Jockey* Queen Anne Press, 1989

If this had happened on grass it would have been unbelievable, but because it is on Fibresand, people think it's a fluke. I don't.

Trainer DAVID BARRON, whose jockey Alex Greaves had ridden 9 winners from her first 14 rides at Southwell, January 1989

I hope that winning the Lincoln will knock on the head the theory that I'm just an all-weather jockey.

ALEX GREAVES after she rode Amenable to a 22/1 Lincoln victory on 23 March 1991

I don't think women jockeys are ever going to be better than men. Women jockeys do a very good job but men are stronger and if you are an owner paying £10,000 a year to keep a horse in training you are going to want the best rider. If I had been neck and neck with Richard Dunwoody going past The Elbow he would have left me 20 lengths behind in the closing straight.

51-year-old ROSEMARY HENDERSON, who finished fifth in the 1994 National on Fiddlers Pike *Daily Telegraph* 11 April 1994

If I had stayed with my husband I would not be training now. He refused to let me do it, so I was determined to prove a point and go it alone. Men feel they are the best trainers. There are not enough of us to compete, but I do admire women trainers like Mary Reveley. It's very tough for us. It's a bloody hard game, like when losing horses in races and on the gallops. But if a woman trainer can take those hammer blows . . . they can take anything.

> Yorkshire trainer SUE BRAMALL *The Sun* 23 April 1994

I was riding so hard and the next thing I knew I was on the floor.

> SARAH BAINBRIDGE who, aged 17, had her first ride on Steel Sovereign at Redcar, winning at 33/1 – and promptly falling off the horse after passing the winning post *Sporting Life* 1 June 1994

Caroline Saunders, three times the champion point-to-point trainer, rode four winners before she was born. Merry Tom conveyed her mother Pam, complete with twins, to win four point-to-points in 1959.

> LUCINDA GREEN on a feat which must have caused a pregnant pause when revealed *Daily Telegraph* 27 April 1994

Fighting the odds

I am proud of my achievements but it always felt as if I was fighting the odds. In the early days even the authorities gave the impression they were against women, to the extent that on many courses facilities were either untenable or non-existent.

Although I achieved several firsts, I never felt as if I was accepted as a jockey in the eyes of the public. Male jockeys were the first to accept me; after a few dirty tricks they saw that I was serious, and although in 1987 some still did not like being beaten by a woman, it had become accepted.

> GAY KELLEWAY, the first female jockey to ride in a Classic and the first to win at Royal Ascot, in *Benson & Hedges Racing Year* Pelham Books, 1989

If she is to carry on her trade without subterfuge she has to have a training licence.

> 1966 Court of Appeal judgement by LORD JUSTICE DENNING on Mrs Florence Nagle which paved the way for women to train legally

The Jockey Club had always shown itself in its silliest mood when refusing to give women the right to hold a licence to train even though it was apparently quite in order for a woman to control a stable providing the actual licence was held by a male underling. The precise reason for this attitude by the Jockey Club was never explained. Perhaps it was just an interesting example of male chauvinism. It was hinted that Weatherbys were distressed at the thought of a woman entering the weighing room and catching a glimpse of a jockey without his trousers on. One normally rational member of the Jockey Club declared that a woman trainer might be influenced by an 'undesirable' man; apparently it was not thought possible that a man could be influenced by an 'undesirable' woman.

ROGER MORTIMER on the refusal to permit women to train until 1996, in *The Flat* George Allen & Unwin, 1979

Despite the successes of Emma O'Gorman and Alex Greaves, it's definitely got a lot tougher for us girls on the Flat. Of the top fifty jockeys in 1993 only Emma was female, but I'm not letting that deter me.

ANTOINETTE ARMES *Sporting Life* 14 April 1994

The only blatant and overt examples [of male chauvinism] have been in the veterinary profession.

LIBBY ARCHER of the Levy Board

I don't feel that any concessions are made to me because I'm a woman. The only difference is you get more kisses and fewer handshakes.

ANNIE DODD, British Horse Racing Industry Committee Executive

The more you see women in racing, the more women will see it as a career.

LUCILLA EVERS, Levy Board lawyer

I don't see any reason why women cannot catch up if they have the ambition.

MORAG GRAY of the RCA

All the above appeared in the Racing Post *21 January 1994*

Darned stupid women jockeys.

First words spoken to jockey Rachel Liron by BRENDAN POWELL when both competed in a race in Jersey which saw Rachel dumped on the way to the start. Their relationship improved though, and they wed in June 1994 *Racing Post* 6 May 1994

It's taken a hell of a long time but it was all worth it.

> Jockey LORNA VINCENT scoring her 100th winner on 1 September 1993, having ridden the first in August 1978

Of course it doesn't pay – but it's my pleasure anyway. There's nothing in the whole world I would rather do.

> Trainer SUE BRAMALL *Racing Post* 3 January 1993

When the jockeys at Newcastle last Saturday decided to wear black armbands in her honour, it was no mere empty gesture but a message from friends sincerely sent.

> JOHN OAKSEY on the reaction to the death of jockey Jayne Thompson *Horse and Hound* 21 November 1986

Small but useful

In a year or two – when the fact of their presence is accepted and the flood of drivelling facetiousness has subsided – they will probably make a small but useful contribution to the racing scene.

> It may sound condescendingly patronising now, but the words of LEN SCOTT in Ruff's Guide on the 1972 introduction of races for women riders could be said to have proved right on the button, even if the 'year or two' was somewhat optimistic

In life I have had all that I really wanted very much – a yacht, a racing stable, a theatre of my own, lovely gardens.

> LILY LANGTRY, who owned two Cesarewitch winners in 1897 and 1908, quoted in *The Fast Set* by George Plumptre/Andre Deutsch, 1985

A woman standing beside me as the runners for the Champion Novice Hurdle were led around the ring said Country Pride would win. I pointed out that all 10 runners carried the name Country Pride on their saddle cloths to acknowledge the Irish backer's sponsorship. She opined that I was a smart ass.

> CLEMENT FREUD *Sporting Life* 27 April 1994

It was just as well I was wearing knickers. Some of the ladies don't.

> Point-to-point rider HELEN PEWTER whose breeches split completely as she fell from Missile Run at Higham in March 1993

I never back a horse that's being led round the paddock by a blonde stable girl. There's no rational explanation – it's a gut feeling.

> A bizarre betting tip from trainer CHARLIE BROOKS whose 'gut feeling' towards blondes is clearly somewhat different from my own. *Daily Mail* 30 April 1994

If I have to limp a little it's worth a trade-off for being able to ride.

> US jock JULIE KRONE on returning to action after a nine-month lay-off following a severe ankle injury *Racing Post* 27 May 1994

Female intuition is involved but between household chores I spend three and a half hours a day studying form.

> Sheffield local paper tipster ANITA BIRCH who hit the national headlines when she tipped 74 winners in 84 days. I gave her £100 to bet with on behalf of a local charity and she found two winners, two seconds and a non-runner in five selections *The Sun* 24 May 1994

TIMELESS QUOTES

National sport

The once national sport of horse racing is being degraded to a trade in which it is difficult to perceive anything either sportive or national . . . The old pretence about the improvement of horses has become a delusion too stale for jesting.

Prime Minister LORD DERBY (died 1869) on the mid-19th-century scandals which rocked the turf

Every great handicap offers a premium to fraud, for horses are constantly started without any intention of winning, merely to hoodwink the handicapper.

Turf administrator ADMIRAL HENRY JOHN ROUS (1795-1877). Has much changed?

We want a man, like Caesar's wife, above suspicion, of independent means, a perfect knowledge of the form and actual conditions of every public horse, without having the slightest interest in any stable.

ADMIRAL ROUS's definition of a public handicapper. And whom did he appoint as public handicapper in 1855? Yes – himself.

Any man who follows the advice of his jockey will soon be ruined.

ADMIRAL ROUS

A mug is born every minute of the day, and thank Gawd some of 'em live.

Early 19th-century bookmaker FRED SWINDELL

I have made the discovery that without guilt or offence I might perpetually run second or third, or even run last, but it becomes a matter of torture to many consciences if I win.

Prime Minister LORD ROSEBERY, whose Ladas won the Derby in 1894

Here lieth the perfect and beautiful symmetry of the much-lamented Highflyer, by whom and his wonderful offspring the celebrated Tattersall acquired a noble fortune, but was not ashamed to acknowledge it.

> Tribute by thoroughbred dealer MR TATTERSALL on the memorial stone of Highflyer, the greatest horse of the late 18th century

In 1773 I could ride horses in a better manner in a race than any person ever known in my time, and in 1775 I could train horses for running better than any person I ever yet saw.

> Modest assessment of his own abilities by Classic-winning SAMUEL CHIFNEY Senior in his 1795 autobiography *Genius Genuine* which, even then, cost £5

It is always convenient but it is not always pleasant.

> JOHN GULLY, the first great and respectable bookmaker, on settling his enormous debts following the crooked coup which saw Matilda win the 1827 St Leger

Better my hat than my head.

> The above-mentioned GULLY following a duel with one Squire Osbaldeston, whose aim was slightly askew

Just put on it 'From Gurry to God'.

> Trainer MARTIN GURRY, whose Sainfoin had just won the Derby (1890), and who had decided to give a thanksgiving gift of a communion plate to his local church at Newmarket

Infamous bookmaker, gambler, owner and trainer Bob Sievier, who owned the immortal Sceptre, winner of every 1902 Classic bar the Derby, once took exception to being described by a newspaper as 'a gambler pure and simple'. He stormed up to the editor and declared: 'I may be pure, but I'm damned if I'm simple.'

I regret I cannot leave Kelso without regretting my not arriving there in time to see the races, which had been the preceding week. These are founded not on the sordid principles of gaming, or dissipation, or fraud, but the beautiful basis of benevolence and with an amiable view of conciliating the affections of two nations.

> THOMAS PENNANT *Tour of Scotland* 1772

For those lucky enough to survive I suppose it was, in a way, a wonderful experience. At least I reckon to know roughly how a horse must feel after being given a really hard race.

> 79-year-old trainer BILL WIGHTMAN who spent three and a half years in a Japanese prisoner of war camp in Sarawak, Borneo, during the Second World War *Daily Telegraph* October 1993

What did I Tulyar?

> Winning jockey CHARLIE SMIRKE after winning the 1952 Derby on Tulyar

If ever the Devil wants to learn a few more diabolical, dirty, villainous tricks he need only attend one or two flapping meetings. They are the last word and quintessence of double-crossing and those who can hold their own at the game make the Devil look like an amateur. They could give the Devil 21lb and a beating.

> Anonymous Scottish owner discussing illegal race meetings in the early 1920s

Famous jockey George Fordham (1937–87) upset temperamental owner the Duchess of Montrose who told him: 'You can hand in my colours, Fordham. You will never ride for me again.' Replied the exasperated Fordham: 'Will your grace stay where she is for a few seconds till I get your colours from the weighing room? I'd like your grace to have them now lest your grace changes her mind.'

They all come to me on bicycles and leave in Bentleys.

> Owner of a large string of horses in the mid 20th century, MAJOR LIONEL HOLLIDAY, discussing his trainers

The best horse I have ever trained, the best I am ever likely to train.

> Trainer FRED DARLING on Hurry On, born 1913. Only raced as a three-year-old, winning all six of his races, including the St Leger. Darling trained seven Derby winners

If I were you I would not bet, but if you must bet – BET!

> Trainer WILLIAM I'ANSON (died 1881) to his eldest son

The stewards did not exchange hats, nor did the bookmakers pay out any bonuses.

> The *Bloodstock Breeders Review* report on the occasion on 8 May 1945 when VE Day coincided with the 1000 Guineas at Newmarket, showing that some things remain the same regardless of outside circumstances

Eclipse first, the rest nowhere.

> The famous bet which became an immortal phrase describing the
> brilliance of the first great racehorse, Eclipse, whose owner DENNIS
> O'KELLY made the bet at Epsom on 3 May 1769. To win the bet, Eclipse
> had to win by so far that the opposition would not even be officially
> placed. He won by a furlong.

I'm afraid my luck is beginning to run out.

> Huge owner PRINCE ALY KHAN in May 1960 after his Sheshoon stumbled
> and lost when looking sure to win at Longchamp. Four days later the
> Prince died in a car crash.

There's three things I can confess to. Since I was 21 I have been
drunk almost every night; I never sold a race, which is more than
some can say; and I never kissed a lass against her will.

> Recorded by contemporary sources as the last words of 50-year-old
> jockey BILL SCOTT who died in 1848 with 19 Classic victories to his
> credit. Of his three confessions, two were reckoned somewhat dubious.

Racing is just like dram-drinking; momentary excitement and
wretched intervals; full consciousness of the mischievous effects of
the habit and equal difficulty in abstaining from it.

> MR CHARLES GREVILLE (1794-1865), owner of Classic winners Preserve
> (1835 1000 Guineas) and Mango (1937 St Leger)

Racing there is run by gentlemen and I am treated like a lady, not
like a business corporation.

> Formerly American owner MRS CHARLES ISELIN (1868-1970) in 1950,
> deciding to switch her interests to England

You may put all the brains you have into racing but you will be
nowhere unless you have luck.

> MAJOR EUSTACE 'LUCKY' LODER (1867-1914) who owned 1000 Guineas,
> Oaks and St Leger winner Pretty Polly

THE SPORT OF KINGS?

Exceptional times

It may be a variety of things that produce exceptional times. The grass management may be different or superior, and it is possible that the horses are much fitter than they used to be. This year's Guineas races were run in unseasonably fast conditions, and that would have an obvious bearing on times. But, as with human athletes, there have been improvements in training methods and the understanding of diets has moved away from the old half a dozen eggs and a pint of Guinness theory.

> British Horseracing Board Handicapper MATTHEW TESTER propounding his slightly bizarre theory that horses are running faster but aren't as good as their predecessors *Pacemaker & Thoroughbred Breeder* June 1994

It is possible that English racing will never be the same again. If there really are long-term implications they are uncomfortable for most Classic-aspiring trainers.

> SIMON BARNES, considering the impact of Balanchine's Oaks victory, having been wintered in Dubai *The Times* 6 June 1994

I certainly think the racing industry would be wise not to be seen to be permanently demanding something else from government.

> Driving force behind the introduction of Sunday racing, JIM PAICE, MP *Pacemaker & Thoroughbred Breeder* June 1994

In the first couple of years nobody from the racing industry made any attempt whatsoever to get to know this new man who was supposed to represent them in Parliament.

> JIM PAICE, MP for Cambridgeshire South East, showing his 'astonishment' at racing's lack of interest in him in his early days in the House *Pacemaker & Thoroughbred Breeder* June 1994

I'm all for progress but there are some aspects of racing that need to be preserved. At the moment we have old expertise integrated with new ideas, some from outside racing. That is important. But parts of racing, like its glamour and mystique, need to be preserved. I will be disappointed if racing becomes a circus or gambling fair.

> Faintly off-beat views from DAVID GIBSON, President of the Thoroughbred Breeders Association *Pacemaker & Thoroughbred Breeder* June 1994

Outside hardcore racegoers, it is very difficult to get people to go racing. Betting shops are much better than they were; television is much improved. The only future for racecourses is to be entertainment centres.

> Interesting conclusion by SIR EVELYN DE ROTHSCHILD, retiring Chairman of United Racecourses *Racing Post* 5 May 1994

We can evaluate yearlings and indicate whether physiologically they are potentially winners or likely also-rans.

> DR ALAN WILSON of Bristol University's sports medicine centre which turned its attentions to racehorses *The Times* 31 December 1993

Britain's greatest enemy today is the do-gooder. They cause havoc in so many walks of life. In our sport, it is often people who know nothing about horses spouting off on what's right and wrong for its well-being.

> Dorset trainer JOHN WEBBER *Racing Post* 6 April 1994

Every problem in the industry can be traced back to the root cause of too many horses. The future of racing is in our own hands. We have the simple choice between selectivity and open-air bingo.

> Opinion of PETER SCOTT, 'Hotspur' of the *Daily Telegraph* for 25 years, recalled in his obituary in that paper on 6 April 1994

The antithesis of all that the phrase classless society represents.

> Description of the Jockey Club by the House of Commons Home Affairs Committee on Gambling and the Tote, in 1991

I would like the public to have more access to the stars in racing – the jockeys, trainers and owners. I would like to see them all spend a few minutes signing autographs and talking to the punters.

> Independent bookmaker WARWICK BARTLETT, Chairman of the British Betting Office Association *Sporting Life* 30 December 1993. Might as well search for Utopia.

Outside hardcore racegoers, it is very difficult to get people to go racing

Always remember that racing is meant to be fun.

> GEOFFREY FREER, Jockey Club handicapper in the early 1940s

I am now confident that Criminal Prosecution Service will not hesitate to prosecute if conspiracy, theft or fraud is shown.

> ROGER BUFFHAM on his campaign to persuade the CPS to regard horse nobbling as an act of criminal conspiracy *Daily Mail* 15 December 1993

Racing has to attract paying customers, and the colour of their money is the same irrespective of the colour of their skin.

> Jamaican-born GODFREY ANDERSON whose company TeleConnection (UK) announced a three-year St Leger sponsorship deal *Racing Post* 27 January 1994

The jockeys' championship? There is no championship any more. Not as we all know it anyway, because the goalposts have been moved. And personally, I don't think it's good for racing.

> Former champion MICHAEL ROBERTS on the year-long flat season *Racing Post* 24 March 1994

A new era

All-year-round racing is something you've got to accept; we're into a new era now.

> Reigning champion PAT EDDERY on the year-long flat season *Racing Post* 24 March 1994

I think the all-weather should be restricted to trainers and jockeys who don't get 50 winners during the normal flat season.

> Trainer IAN BALDING *Today* 25 March 1994

You are lucky not to have it yet in England. When it arrives you will see what damage it causes.

> LOUIS ROMANET of France's racing authority GIE-Galop on the National Lottery *Sporting Life* 26 January 1994

It all comes down to speed on the phone, spotting the best ride and getting on it. I don't go round jocking people off their regular rides, but every other ride is up for grabs.

> Clear statement of intent from agent DAVE ROBERTS *The Times* 8 April 1994

This death is the culmination of increasing racecourse violence. Something like this was certain to happen. There were two coach-loads of yobs who were allowed into the course and this was a straightforward example of the worst kind of football hooliganism being transferred from the terraces to the racecourse. They were not real racegoers and were only interested in being able to drink all day and cause trouble.

> Reported comments of a police spokesman after a 24-year-old man was murdered in a coach-park brawl involving 70 yobs at Newmarket in August 1988. Police retained 40 people. Ruff's Guide; *Sporting Life* 1989

Everyone involved in the administration of racing must learn from this horrific incident and ensure they act as a matter of urgency.

> JOCKEY CLUB statement in response to the above. Fortunately, the lessons of that incident seem largely to have been learned, although there are still occasional unfortunate outbreaks

The betting shop demand for racing every day will be met by all-weather racing

It is likely that within 10 years British racing will operate on three tiers.

The betting shop demand for racing every day will be met by all-weather racing, much of it under floodlights. The leading 10 or 12 courses will share the resources available, offering superb facilities and high prize-money. The remaining courses will race in the evenings and at weekends, catering primarily for a local market.

JOCELYN DE MOUBRAY *Pacemaker & Thoroughbred Breeder* May 1994

If the Tote wishes to win the confidence of punters it needs to do several things. It needs to reduce its expenditure on entertainment and self-indulgence because punters know it's their money being used. It needs to declare its pools on each race and on each type of bet so punters can see exactly where the money has gone. In the event of an apparently anomalous dividend it needs to go out of its way to apologise and to explain why the payout is so low.

It also needs an off-course monopoly. But it doesn't have much chance of getting one while it does so little to persuade us it deserves it.

Arch-champion of the Tote monopolists, PAUL HAIGH, seeming to lose a little enthusiasm for the object of his own desire *Racing Post* 13 May 1994

I have little time for horseracing. It is controlled by members of a certain class with a certain level of wealth. They run it as a private club.

> Labour MP for Liverpool Walton, PETER KILFOYLE *Sporting Life* 11 May 1994

The speed of the horses, the unsuitable surface and the demands of the new obstacle.

> Reasons cited for scrapping all-weather-hurdling by PAUL GREEVES, British Horseracing Board Racing Director

The emphasis today is not on stamina but speed – and greed.

> CAPTAIN JOHN ROUND-TURNER, Director of the National Horseracing Museum in Newmarket, on how much shorter are today's races than those of yore (*Daily Telegraph* 23 April 1994). With admission at £3.30 at time of going to press and with plenty to see, perhaps the Museum is practising what it preaches!

I write as one of the only journalists who, in a previous existence as rider and public trainer, has actually been first knocked out of a race on a hot favourite, and secondly, on two occasions been offered bribes of substantial money and nubile girls to ensure that favourites did not win.

> TIM FITZGEORGE-PARKER, who presumably didn't think it was worth mentioning to anyone at the time! *Raceform Update* September 1993

What next?

I can honestly see the time when there won't be any jump racing, or only a very limited amount as in the US and Australia. People are anti-whips, anti-jumps, what next?

> MARTIN PIPE (*Sporting Life* 26 February 1994) arguing that stopping all-weather hurdling is the thin end of the wedge

Racing is losing much of its popularity with the general public in Britain.

> J.A. McGRATH *Sporting Life* 28 February 1994

The Jockey Club stifled innovation and enterprise and rarely initiated anything worthwhile.

> 'Racehorses of 1993' *Timeform*

I stressed that applicants must be keen workers to help in the yard as well. As soon as you mention work, no one wants to know.

> Trainer ALF SMITH who advertised without a single reply for an apprentice to take most of the stable rides *Sporting Life* 26 February 1994

To describe all-weather jumping as carnage is cobblers.

> DAVID PIPE of the Jockey Club responding to a question from *Today*'s Colin Cameron *Today* 26 February 1994

Starting is one of the arts of jockeyship and it would be a very sad day for jump racing if they ever brought starting stalls in.

> OLIVER SHERWOOD, interviewed by Marcus Armytage in the *Daily Telegraph*

I can see a time in the future when jumping goes back to being a point-to-point pastime because there aren't enough horses to fill the racing calendar.

> RON MUDDLE, owner of Southwell and Wolverhampton racecourses *Daily Mail* 23 November 1993

Infection can be carried in the wind.

> TIM FITZGEORGE-PARKER quoting Luca Cumani and fearing an outbreak of equine disease *Raceform Update* 11 December 1993

Annus mediocris.

> MICHAEL BYRNE, Classifications Committee Chairman, commenting on the International Classifications for 1993

To ban the whip would be like asking a sailor to steer a boat without a rudder.

> JENNY PITMAN (*The Observer* 30 January 1994)

This sort of performance is thumbing the nose at authority, spitting on the public and bringing British racing into disrepute.

> TIM FITZGEORGE-PARKER berating trainers for schooling in public *Raceform Update* October 1993

Punters are being taken for a ride when they back horses that are not fit – and some trainers run their charges at a level of fitness that does not allow them to run at their best.

You do not see many fat athletes and fat horses do not win many races.

> PETER SCUDAMORE *Daily Mail* October 1993

Cissy stuff.

ISOBEL CUNNINGHAM of *The Scotsman* on all-weather racing *The Scotsman* 20 January 1994

But, exactly, what defines a winning distance? Most people will say the distance back to the second as the winner passes the line. But what if the eventual runner-up is a length or two back in third as the winner actually passes the line?

The only truly accurate record of any type of race is in the finishing times of the competitors and since 1952 the photo-finish negative has been able to show a time for every horse, either absolute for courses with electronic timing, or relative to the winner for the majority of tracks that don't boast that facility.

Why not just measure the distance back on the photo-finish visually?

Logical sounding suggestion by TONY HARBIDGE *Racing Post* 20 April 1994

It could be used as a licence to cheat with a horse; let it run below form, provide an excuse, lump the money down next time out, win 10 lengths and there will be nothing said about it.

PETER CUNDELL of the National Trainers Federation on Jockey Club plans to demand public explanations when horses run unaccountably badly. Was he being serious?

What a pleasure to see Flakey Dove storm home in the Champion Hurdle without the Chancellor of the Exchequer trying to creep up on her inside. Year after year, Chancellors would time their budgets for Cheltenham week and I would object to them for bumping and boring. Mine was an uphill effort, but at last it got home. Norman Lamont's budgets were the last of their kind and the least that Cheltenham's graceless management can do is to name a race in his honour.

CHRISTOPHER FILDES on the removal of the tradition linking the Budget speech to Cheltenham *The Spectator* 19 March 1994

There should be no place in a championship race for moderate horses and, with that in mind, I would suggest a minimum rating requirement for all such races so that the best are allowed to take on the best without hindrance.

SIMON HOLT *Sporting Life* 21 March 1994. Bit eletist, what?

If the British Horseracing Board and Jockey Club wish to create a flat racing championship meeting, they will have to give serious consideration to moving the Derby to later in the season and taking steps to ensure that other races over a variety of distances are staged at the same time.

MICHAEL WAUDBY of Brough, East Yorkshire, letter to *The Times* 24 March 1994

Endangered species

Kemp's Ridley Sea Turtle, the Conondale Gastric Brooking Frog and the Scimitar-Horned Oryx are among earth's most endangered species, according to the World Conservation Union, who have identified 6000 creatures at risk. Yet the equine cognoscenti are puzzled that the rarest mammal in Europe – the Northern Classic Winner – is not listed.

A few years ago it could be glimpsed rarely if infrequently; Waterloo travelled south from Bill Watts' Richmond Yard in 1972 to land a notable success in the 1000 Guineas, and five years later Mick Easterby's Mrs McArdy won the same race. But with no sighting during the subsequent 17 years, the breed was considered to be extinct.

GRAHAM ROCK shortly before Mr Baileys, trained 'oop in t'north o' t'country', won the 1994 2000 Guineas *The Observer* 24 April 1994. Next, the return of Nessie?

Jockeys should work harder to understand horses. They use the whip rather than ride them out properly, and often get unbalanced. I think we've got a logical attitude. I can't see any objection to letting jockeys carry a whip provided they keep their hands on the reins and use it in the back hand to slap a horse down the shoulder.

There didn't seem to be anything wrong with the surface or the equipment. It's speed that kills, jockeys going too fast.

I'm a great believer in hybrid vigour. Of course, the very suggestion will upset the purists, but I'm sure that in-breeding produces unsoundness in the long run.

The above views (on whips, all-weather jumping and in-breeding) were expressed by the Royal Society for the Prevention of Cruelty to Animals equine consultant BERNARD DONIGAN *The Observer* 3 April 1994

It is notorious that racing in Great Britain has for more than a generation been a ruinously expensive pastime, and the marvel is that the public have tolerated the excessive charges they were called upon to pay.

> Contemporary? Could be, but isn't – *Bloodstock Breeders' Review* 1929

The hope is entertained that the barbarous practice of firing horses will soon be entirely abandoned.

> *Bloodstock Breeders' Review* 1927. Firing continues today, despite being outlawed in the early 1990s. The cauterising of legs to strengthen the tissues (firing) was recorded as long ago as 1677.

There are an awful lot of people there that seem to be against change just because they want to be against change. I have certainly got the impression that many of the vested interests in racing would have been happier if we had simply put up the money and shut up and not bothered about a creche, hot air balloons, marching bands, pop concerts and a tented village.

That is considered to be not what it is all about. Well, we consider it is very much what it is all about.

We need racecards that can be understood by normal human beings. We need facilities for children. We need a day at the races to become good value and family entertainment. If we don't achieve that, in 50 years' time they will say, 'Did you know, they used to train horses in Newmarket?'

We are just seen as Johnny-come-latelies who have got above our station. We have little in mind for providing facilities for racing aficionados who will be coming anyway to enjoy first-class racing, and we could not care less about providing facilities for people who don't pay to get in because they are part of the racing establishment.

> Some admirable feather-ruffling from BERNARD GOVER, Managing Director of debt collectors Madagans, whose efforts to beef up the entertainment value of the Newmarket meeting at which they sponsor the 1000 and 2000 Guineas met with less than wholehearted approval. Well, *what* a surprise! *The Times* 27 April 1993

As far as money is concerned, sport in the UK is dominated by athletics, football and horseracing. But world-wide, Britons are richer from playing golf and driving fast cars.

> Business-Age magazine (May 1994), which rated Lester Piggott the sixth richest sportsman in Britain (£13m), with Pat Eddery tenth (£7.25m) and Willie Carson fourteenth (£6.65m).

The nonsense of making highly-strung horses parade before big races.

> MONTY COURT's controversial opinion that 'thoroughbreds are bred to race, not to parade' Sporting Life 29 April 1994

We cannot completely eliminate the risk which is at the heart of racing.

> DR MICHAEL TURNER, Jockey Club medical adviser, unveiling a new design of crash helmet The Times 6 May 1994

The Big Three do a good marketing job for racing as a whole, and the state of the industry in this country compares well with countries such as France where there is a Tote monopoly.

> William Hill Managing Director JOHN BROWN, replying to criticism that racing could not prosper while the Big Three bookmakers dominated the betting industry Sporting Life 11 May 1994

The government of this country thinks London is the centre of the earth and horseracing has gone down the same road. The whole country has suffered over a long period of time from centralisation, and, in racing, this has snowballed and a lot of trainers lost confidence as they lost horses.

> MARK JOHNSTON, beating the drum for the north after sending out their first 2000 Guineas winner for some 30 years, Mr Baileys The Independent 3 April 1994

There are those who denounce the progress of recent years. For them, racing is already too commercial, too populist, too willing to pander to the needs of the masses. They would rather the serenity of a deserted racecourse, as though their horses were still competing in the age of the private sweepstake.

> JULIAN MUSCAT The Times 16 May 1994

An English racecourse during the summer is no longer a suitable place for a young child

An English racecourse during the summer is no longer a suitable place for a young child.

At the 2000 Guineas meeting at Newmarket, young men were wandering around the members' enclosure with lager bottles in hand. On the top floor of the members' stand there was panic caused by the crush before the big race.

At Bath, Haydock and Chester there are summer days – during the football recess – when Tattersalls is akin to the terraces of football clubs. Unfortunately, many people equate going racing with getting drunk.

> A bleak view of race-going by JULIAN WILSON in an interview with Sue Montgomery *Independent on Sunday* 15 May 1994

Racing's got a really old-fashioned image. Young people want glamour and novelty. It's way too expensive to get in and it's hard to know what's going on if you're not an insider . . . The courses are full of upper-class idiots and dress restrictions. It's not what the young want.

> RICHARD BENSON of style-conscious, trendy *The Face* magazine *Racing Post* 18 May 1994. To be ignored at the sport's peril.

For too long racing has failed to see itself as others see it – a myste-
rious world of arcane rituals, expensive, old-fashioned and
privileged, with a whiff of the seedy to boot.

> *Sporting Life* editorial 18 May 1994

Racing, or rather the British Horseracing Board, must make up its
collective mind. If it really believes that the financial viability of the
sport depends, through betting turnover, on a vast and growing
number of fixtures, it must also face the fact that programmes will
only be published on a selective basis – a basis which would soon
lead to the concept of 'second-class racing'.

> JOHN OAKSEY 'greeting' the news that the British Horseracing Board's
> 1995 fixture list contained 'no less than 1170 meetings' and warning
> that newspapers might well begin to decline the opportunity of carrying
> full details of all of them *Sporting Life* 21 May 1994

If racing isn't a spectator sport, it's nothing.

> British Horseracing Board supremo TRISTRAM RICKETTS *MoS* 22 May 1994

An insane decision . . . madness, born out of greed and a misguided
view of what is desired by racing's customers, on and off-course.

It would make more sense if the jumps season ended with the
Whitbread Gold Cup at Sandown towards the end of April and,
similarly, the domestic flat season drew to a close after the
Champion Stakes meeting at Newmarket in the middle of October.

> RICHARD EVANS on plans to introduce summer jump racing *The Times* 23
> May 1994

No holiday next summer.

> RICHARD DUNWOODY's reaction to the news of summer jumping *Sporting
> Life* 23 May 1994

In the last 20 years, racing has done very little to change itself in a
way that catches the breath. You could look at any other sport and
see examples of this. What we need is a European grand prix season
for horses, as they have in athletics. We all lament the way our best
three-year-olds are rushed off to stud, yet collectively we have not
done anything about it.

> ANDREW FRANKLIN, producer of *Channel 4 Racing*. And who would televise
> this grand prix, I wonder? *The Times* 28 May 1994

THE DERBY – NOW AND THEN

An eventful race

The Derby 1994 . . . An eventful race with 25 runners, much jostling, a fall from Foyer by Willie Ryan and victory for Willie Carson on Erhaab with a breathtaking late charge to overhaul King's Theatre and Colonel Collins.

It was carnage out there with so many runners jostling for position and they were lucky that only one horse came down. They just should not allow so many bad horses to run. They only get in the way.

> WILLIE CARSON *Daily Mirror* 2 June 1994

Moderate horses on paper have won the Derby and if the owner has spent money entering a horse for the Derby and the trainer can't stop him from being stupid they should have the opportunity to run.

> JOHN DUNLOP, winning trainer *The Times* 2 June 1994

I know the owners pay the money to enter, but it is distracting from the good horses.

> WILLIE CARSON *The Times* 2 June 1994

I'm here to show the ordinary punter that this needn't be the sport of kings. If you have a horse you can run it in the Derby. I think I was more excited than he was. If I'd have won I'd have been doing somersaults over the rails.

> Owner of tailed-off-last Plato's Republic, TOMMY LONG, who shook hands with winning owner Sheikh Al Maktoum after the race *The Times* 2 June 1994

You know, that's the best race he's ever run.

> Said not of the winner, but of the *last*, by his trainer JOHN JENKINS *The Times* 2 June 1994

It was bloody ridiculous. The worst and roughest race I have ever ridden in.

> MICHAEL ROBERTS, unplaced on Ionio

There were five or six horses almost tailed off after four furlongs. That meant there were less than 20 in the race when Foyer was bumped. So, if you restrict the size of the field, where do you draw the line?

> BARRY HILLS *The Times* 2 June 1994

The race was rough. But look at the outcome. The best horse won. For all our problems in running it made not the slightest difference in the end.

> JOHN REID *The Times* 2 June 1994

There was a problem with the number of horses. The question of the standard of horses is a wider issue.

> Epsom Clerk of the Course MICHAEL WEBSTER *Daily Express* 2 June 1994

There were far too many bad horses.

> MICHAEL HILLS, whose Broadway Flyer ran like one of them

I had written off Erhaab because he was so far behind.

> Trainer JOHN DUNLOP

It was certainly one of the best rides I can remember a jockey giving in the race.

> PETER SCUDAMORE on Willie Carson *Daily Mail* 2 June 1994

What he did was, quite simply, rode the race of his life.

> *Daily Express* chief sports writer JAMES LAWTON

I seriously doubt if many other jockeys in living memory would have won on Erhaab.

> ALASTAIR DOWN *Sporting Life*

A Derby ride that many who witnessed it will argue was the greatest in history.

ROY COLLINS, chief sports writer, *Today*

The man is mad, of course. To slalom through a stampede of wild horses just below Tattenham Corner on a June afternoon by choice when you are 51 years old and can damned nearly buy the place is the very definition of insanity.

IAN WOOLDRIDGE *Daily Mail* 2 June 1994

As much like the Clitheroe Kid as ever.

MATTHEW ENGEL on Willie Carson *The Guardian*. If you don't know, ask your Dad!

Bloody hell!

Carson's reaction when he realised that he had the best part of a furlong to make up on Master Baileys *The Independent*

Us Grandads did all right, didn't we.

WILLIE CARSON on the performance of himself and fellow grandfather Piggott, who was fifth

I've ridden in Australia and jockeys were doing things that would get them stood down for a year out there.

> KIERAN FALLON who rode Party Season (15th)

It is easy to refer to him as a black bullet, but he is *not* black. There is enough tan on his muzzle to put him in the brown category, and he is registered as such, but the last horse as dark as him to win the Derby was Grand Parade in 1919 and he *was* officially black.

> Breeding expert SUE MONTGOMERY not quite blackening Erhaab's name
> *Racing Post*

The name Erhaab has a thousand different meanings in Arabic, but the nearest I could give you to English is strong and brave.

> Erhaab's owner, SHEIKH HAMDAN AL MAKTOUM *Sporting Life*

This morning I woke up thinking to myself, where am I going today – Folkestone?

> Self-mocking comment by LESTER PIGGOTT reported by Lord Oaksey
> *Sporting Life*

It was great for me but I don't know how the horse felt about it.

> DARREN BIGGS, rider of last horse, Plato's Republic *Sporting Life*

He seemed rather well endowed.

> Anonymous woman racegoer commenting not on the stud prospects of the winner but on the Derby streaker.

Nobody has asked her. I expect we'll find out in due course.

> The Queen's Racing Manager, EARL OF CARNARVON, asked by Ross Benson, *Daily Express* gossip columnist, for the Queen's thoughts on a Sunday Derby *Daily Express*

Tell them Mr Binstock remembers Pearl Harbor. No deal!

> Owner of Derby fancy Broadway Flyer, FREDDY BINSTOCK, when told by his trainer John Hulls that a Japanese syndicate was prepared to bid £1 million for the horse *Daily Star* 1 June 1994

The Queen's Stand, which was surely assembled from the old parts of an unwanted Russian cruise ship.

> ROBERT PHILIP *Daily Telegraph* 3 June 1994

I wish they could devise a plan to eliminate no-hopers in the Derby. It was a rough race and those who run just because they wish to see their colours in the Blue Riband, in my opinion, are doing nobody any favours and [I] regard them as having little respect for the race itself.

> Pretty elitist stuff from HENRY CECIL *Sporting Life* 4 June 1994

I guarantee you that was one of the roughest races I have ever ridden in.

> WALTER SWINBURN *Sporting Life* 4 June 1994

No one wants as many as 33, which is the upper limit currently allowed, but settling for a quorum of stars, presumably owned by the Maktoums and Sangsters of the game, would irretrievably diminish the occasion.

> HUGH McILVANNEY *Sunday Times* 5 June 1994

Long before anyone gets frightened into limits it seems to me that the jockeys themselves would do well to examine the film of it frame by frame. In Australia the stewards would have done that – and one or two sizeable suspensions might well have been awarded.

> LORD OAKSEY *Daily Telegraph* 4 June 1994

It would be amusing after the Derby, especially if he'd won it, to say, well, that's got him nicely wound-up for the Finale Junior Hurdle at Chepstow.

> Trainer ROBIN DICKIN, pondering on the chances of his 1000/1 Epsom no-hoper Colonel Colt, 12 days before the Derby which the horse, surprise, surprise, didn't win (*The Independent* 20 May 1994). I wonder how he got on in the Finale Junior Hurdle?

You need a crystal ball to know your Derby horse in early March. For me, there's no doubt that the lack of a late entry degrades the race.

> RICHARD HANNON calling for a later supplementary stage for the Blue Riband *The Times* 18 May 1994

I remember a few years ago, a horse wasn't entered for the Derby and everyone said it would have a big chance but instead it went to the French Derby and started favourite. I said some very uncharacteristic prayers in church that morning and, sure enough, it got soundly stuffed.

> United Racecourses Managing Director TIM NELIGAN, pouring scorn on anxieties about three of 1994's recognised Derby trials winners missing the race and thus devaluing the form *The Independent* 25 May 1994

This highlight of the flat racing season has increasingly become the province for corporate hospitality, with the charabancs of ordinary punters being marginalised.

> JOHN GOODBODY on TV sport in *The Times* 28 May 1994

We're looking for £1.5 million annually for exclusive sponsorship of the meeting including the Oaks and the Coronation Cup.

> RHT Managing Director DAVID HILLYARD, spelling out his terms for sponsorship of the 1995 Derby meeting – take it out of petty cash, old boy! *Daily Telegraph* 25 May 1994

Professionals will be more than welcome, but we hope the tourists who visit Hampton Court and Buckingham Palace will also venture out to see the home of the Derby.

> United Racecourses' TIM NELIGAN on Epsom's Ever Ready Derby Hall of Fame, an attraction unveiled in June 1994 but, with a breathtaking ability to spot a potential audience, *closed* on Derby Day and all other race days *Sporting Life* 25 May 1994

Surrounded as he is by increasingly more technical equipment, it is a peculiar fact that Franklin, 43, will not see a racehorse in the flesh all day. Not many people know that!

> JULIAN MUSCAT writing in *The Times* of 28 May 1994 about *Channel 4 Racing*'s producer Andrew Franklin's Derby Day activities

The crowds at Melbourne don't see the race. They go for the party. We've lost that here. There's no longer an identify between public and race. The Derby's lost its legend.

> Cheltenham boss EDWARD GILLESPIE comparing the Melbourne Cup with the Derby and apparently suggesting that the Derby would be better served by attracting people who don't want to see the race! *Sporting Life* 29 May 1994

It takes two days to put down 120 two-inch thick coconut mats. They are made by people at a blind school in London.

> Head groundsman at Epsom, SEAMUS BUCKLEY, explaining how the four roads which cross the Derby course are covered *Sporting Life* 30 May 1994

I don't see any reason why I shouldn't be back next year – or even the year after that.

> LESTER PIGGOTT raising the interesting possibility that he could eventually become the first pensioner to ride the winner of the Derby *MoS* 29 May 1994

God knows, you've got no chance with a race like the Derby. The bastards are all trying.

> Anonymous head lad's warning to writer JEFFREY BERNARD, reported by John Karter in *Sunday Times* 25 May 1994

It was just another race.

> LESTER PIGGOTT to reporters after riding Never Say Die to win the Derby – his first win in the race (1954)

When Gay Time threw me it was probably his way of telling me I rode a stinker.

> LESTER PIGGOTT after finishing second in the Derby on Gay Time who threw him shortly after passing the post (1952)

I remember somebody asked me how I was going to celebrate after I won my first Derby. I told him I was going home to cut the grass.

> LESTER PIGGOTT *MoS* 29 May 1994

The English and French Derby may clash next year with the possibility of both being run on the first Sunday in June. Certainly the Epsom Classic should be. To launch Sunday betting with the 1995 Derby represents a unique marketing opportunity. I have a name for it – D-DAY II. Why not invite survivors of the Normandy Landings to attend, free of charge? Space should not be a problem; while the big race was being run on Wednesday, there was room for a game of croquet on the members' lawn.

> GRAHAM ROCK *The Observer* 5 June 1994

The Derby itself may be staging a revival, albeit a limited one, but the meeting as a whole is still a desperate affair compared with the Kentucky Derby, the Melbourne Cup or, nearer to home, the Cheltenham Festival. It is not marketed or promoted particularly well and urgently needs new ideas and, above all, new people. The team now running Epsom is, at best, second rate, when compared with the people running York, Doncaster and Goodwood. Who else would spend £500,000 on a Hall of Fame which cannot be open to the public on race days!

RICHARD EVANS *The Times* 6 June 1994 – my thoughts entirely

The memory still lingers

One day it rained, a recession blew away the mystique and Derby Day lost its hold on our senses.

The memory still lingers, as an image of loss, of desertion. It was 1990, and Quest For Fame was spinning round Tattenham Corner and towards the cambered finishing straight. There was no boiling point, no tumult, just swathes of unoccupied downland and a low, tired, rained-on feeling of ordinariness.

The Derby is no longer unmissable. It is as if the nation suddenly caught on to the absurdity of surrendering a Wednesday to the foot-bruising and rib-crushing discomfort of it all. It was another of history's spells broken.

PAUL HAYWARD, 'Talking Sport' in the *Daily Telegraph* 1 June 1994

I would like to see a drastic reduction in entry fees – £1 to enter and £2 to run.

ROBERT SANGSTER's revolutionary Derby entry scheme *Sporting Life* 7 December 1993

The idea is fine as long as the prize money is £100.

TIM NELIGAN, Managing Director of Epsom's owners United Racecourses, answering the above Sangster suggestion *Sporting Life* 7 December 1993

What you have to do is move the Oaks and the Derby on to the same card. Shift the $1^{1}/_{4}$ mile handicap from Derby Day and make it worth £100,000 to the winner. And move the Temple Stakes from

Sandown. This Saturday will then instantly become the biggest racing day of the year.

ROBERT SANGSTER's plan to shift the Derby and Epsom 'back on top where it belongs'

I would prefer a two-day meeting – with the Oaks and Derby on Saturday.

HENRY CECIL

Stuffing four or five Group Ones together doesn't always work.

Epsom Clerk of the Course MICHAEL WEBSTER

I'd take it all by the scruff of the neck and hold it all on one day, the Saturday. You would have the Derby as the centrepiece of your programme, but you would precede it with both the Oaks and the Coronation Cup.

BROUGH SCOTT's proposal for rearranging the Derby meeting, as told to *The Observer*'s Jon Henderson 29 May 1994

In the year 2000, the Derby will be run at 6 a.m. on Sunday 20 August in order to service the peak time of 200,000 Chinese betting shops.

Epsom Managing Director TIM NELIGAN taking a tongue-in-cheek look ahead *Sporting Life* 31 May 1994

I find that people in Japan, Korea and Hong Kong almost stand to attention when they find that I am representing the home of the Derby.

Epsom's Managing Director TIM NELIGAN, who probably didn't get quite the same reaction over here! *Sporting Life* 31 May 1994

I do not expect to win

I do not mind confessing that I do not expect to win – but I cannot see anything that is going to beat me.

LORD DERBY, prior to the 1929 Derby in which his Hunter's Moon finished – fourth

If he wins, I'm dead.

> Very much alive EWAN ANDERSON, manager of the only betting shop in
> Tenby, on the eve of the 1993 Derby, before hot favourite Tenby was
> well beaten

It is reported that the head of one of the greatest Derby winners of
all time, Sea Bird II, was discovered in a dustbin at a knackers yard.

> TIM FITZGEORGE-PARKER *Raceform Update* 29 January 1994

Hoary reprobate.

> Contemporary description of Lord Clermont, owner of Aimwell, winner
> of the 1785 Derby

Depend on it, that Eleanor is the hell of a mare.

> The dying words of trainer COX who passed on shortly before Eleanor
> duly won the 1801 Derby

The lowest and longest and most double-jointed horse, with the
best legs and the worst feet I ever saw.

> Stud groom for the Duke of Grafton, DRYMAN, on the 1810 winner,
> Whalebone

Buckle and I wound in and out all the way from Tattenham Corner
like a dog at a fair.

> 1821 winning jockey SAM DAY who partnered Gustavus while Buckle was
> on runner-up Reginald. They had to negotiate a way through the out of
> control crowd which surged on to the course.

Even with five gallons inside, nothing would touch him.

> Trainer EDWARDS after discovering that 1825 favourite Middleton had
> been nobbled just before the race by being given a bucket of water to
> drink. Edwards was right; Middleton won by two lengths.

'Tis over, the trick for the thousands is done
George Edwards on Phosphorous the Derby has won.

> Excellent piece of tipping by VATES in *Bells Life* just prior to the 1837
> Derby, won by Phosphorous at 40/1

A thousand pounds for a pull!

> Reported desperate offer by BILL SCOTT, riding favourite and runner-up
> Launcelot in the 1840 Derby, to winning jockey MacDonald on 50/1
> chance Little Wonder, who apparently replied: 'Too late, Mr Scott, too
> late!'

Thank God I've won the Derby – and not a soul is on but myself!

> Literally a classic case of speaking too soon, for MR DRINKALD, the owner of 200/1 outsider Black Tommy, was devastated when 20/1 shot Blink Bonny, who had finished neck and neck with his horse, was declared the winner of the 1857 race

It is not generally known that Lord Lyon was a very slight whistler, and was fired with a flat iron on his throat by Stanley, the veterinary surgeon of Leamington, who just then believed in that treatment. Whether it did him any good or not I can't say.

> Nor, presumably, could the horse, on whom HENRY CUSTANCE won the 1866 Derby *Riding Recollections and Turf Stories*, 1894

He bought horses as though he were drunk and backed them as if he were mad.

> Said of Mr Henry, later Lord Chaplin, owner of 1867 winner Hermit

We, as Stewards of Epsom, unanimously decide that the chestnut colt Bend Or, which came in first for the Derby of 1880, is by Doncaster out of Rouge Rose, and therefore the objection lodged by Messrs Brewer and Blanton is overruled.

> Announcement rejecting allegations that the 1880 winner was a 'ringer'

Whatever they have offered you, I'll pay you double if you win.

> Owner BRODERICK CLOETE to his jockey Fred Webb immediately before the 1885 Derby, having heard that Webb had been 'got at'. Webb, riding Paradox, finished second.

He was, for a jockey, about the pluckiest and best rough-horseman I have ever seen, and with it all he was the cheeriest soul imaginable. The natural ready wit of Jones, and his gaiety, together with the absolute trust we had in him, appealed immensely to us all. A better servant no man ever had and a straighter jockey never got on a horse.

> Trainer RICHARD MARSH on Herbert Jones, who rode 1900 Derby winner Diamond Jubilee, owned by the Prince of Wales, and who died, aged 70, in 1951

It's lucky for some of us that Mr George doesn't turn pro.

> Top jockey DANNY MAHER (to be champion jockey) on George Thursby, the only amateur to have ridden a placed horse in the Derby, which he did in 1904 and 1906

I spoke to Williamson on the phone and he was very decent about everything. He will ride for me again, and there are no hard feelings.

American JOHN GALBREATH, owner of 1972 winner Roberto, ridden by Lester Piggott, for whom Bill Williamson had been 'jocked off'

When I won the Derby I was in a helicopter and leaving Epsom within 30 minutes of the weigh-in. It left me with an empty feeling.

MICHAEL KINANE, Commander-In-Chief's jockey, quoted by J.A. McGrath *Daily Telegraph* 15 November 1993

Medical Officer authorises the issue of Champagne to all ranks.

Telegram sent to Commanding Officer of the South Irish Horse regiment after Orby won the 1907 Derby, by its trainer COLONEL FREDERICK McCABE, former Medical Officer to the regiment

Come on Rustom Pasha!

Classic case of mistaken identity as the Aga Khan cheered on his Derby second favourite as it hit the front in the 1930 Derby, only to discover that the horse was actually his second string, 18/1 shot Blenheim, which went on to win

He will win the Derby, but I may not live to see it.

Prophetic words in 1928 by owner-breeder LORD DEWAR of his colt-foal Cameronian who duly won the 1931 Derby in the colours of J.A. Dewar, nephew to his Lordship, who had died in April 1930

Had I ridden him, he would have won on the bit by many lengths. Had any other English jockey, who knew the course, ridden him, he would have won comfortably.

The possibly not entirely unbiased views of STEVE DONOGHUE on the performance of Aussie jockey W.R. Johnstone, who found all sorts of trouble when riding 1934 Derby 11/8 hot favourite Colombo into third place. Donoghue had won on the horse as a two-year-old.

Aye, he goes a bit.

Underwhelmed Yorkshire trainer MATT PEACOCK after his Dante won the 1945 Derby

The turf in Ireland has no spring in it, the climate is too depressing and no Irish trainer knows enough to even dare to compete for the greatest race in the world.

> WILLIAM ALLINSON of *The Sportsman* in 1907 just before Ireland's Orby won the Derby

To adjourn for that day is part of the unwritten law of Parliament.

> LORD PALMERSTON, quoted in 1860 when questioned on whether the House would be taking Derby Day off. How many MPs would like Derby Day off nowadays?

The Stewards were satisfied that no individual was to blame. There was no evidence of rough riding. The general opinion of the jockeys was that too many horses were falling back after six furlongs, and the remainder closed up, and in the general scrimmage some horse was brought down, the rest falling over that horse.

The Stewards accepted that view and regret that such a large number of horses not up to classic standard were allowed by their owners and trainers to start.

> Official statement following 1962 Derby in which seven runners fell during the descent to Tattenham Corner. Twenty-six ran.

The horse fell on the woman and kicked out furiously, and it was sickening to see his hoofs strike her repeatedly. It all happened in a flash. Before we had time to realise it was over. The horse struggled to its feet – I don't think it was hurt – but the jockey and the woman lay on the ground. It was a terrible thing.

> Eye-witness account from the *Manchester Guardian* (June 1913) of the death of militant suffragette Emily Davison, who threw herself at the King's horse during the 1913 Derby

MEDIA MATTERS

The unwitting message

Kevin Mann's film succeeds triumphantly. The unwitting message is about social hierarchy, with the jockeys at the bottom of the pile. Owners and trainers have the posh accents while the jockeys take the hard knocks. It is a short career, modestly rewarded and likely to be littered with injury.

> TV critic PETER WAYMARK on Channel 4's 'Champions: Fit to Ride' *The Times* 2 April 1994

I wonder whether the BBC was looking to achieve some sort of record during its coverage of Thursday at Aintree. The BBC used 10 commentators/pundits – Messrs O'Sullevan, Wilson, McGrath, Hanmer, Rock, Pitman, Smith, Scudamore and Powell, plus Ms Piggott.

> GRAHAM WHITEHOUSE in a letter to the *Racing Post* 12 April 1994

I went on a TV programme and met these rabbity, snotty-nosed, insignificant little girls and boys. These so-called do-gooders – cranks is a better word – got on the back of the National because they get publicity out of it. If it weren't this race it would be something else. Never mind putting horses down, they should put these buggers down.

> GINGER McCAIN on animal rights protestors *Daily Star* 6 April 1994

For four or five nights afterwards I had nightmares. I was even waking up in a cold sweat.

> DEREK THOMPSON on being 'Gotcha-ed' by Noel Edmonds for his *House Party* of 5 February 1994 *Racing Post* 14 January 1994

One has to admire him for his stamina and enthusiasm – he certainly adds a bit of colour, although his dress sense leaves something to be desired.

> Well-known dandy HENRY CECIL, on well-known sartorial disaster area John McCririck *Sporting Life* 7 May 1994

Who is the chap on Channel 4 who really gives you the hump? My choice is the smug announcer who gives us the starting prices for the day's other meetings. When Woodrow's Winner buzzes in at 6/1 at Folkestone or some other gaff and pays £10.20 on the Tote, he announces to the world what a great divvy the nanny has paid.

But five minutes later a result comes in from Ripon and Mugs Are Us has obliged at 3/1, but only pays £2.50 on the Tote.

Does the same chirpy chappie inform us of the dreadful payout that Tote customers have received? You can have 100–1 with me he does.

> MARK WINSTANLEY exposes a Tote-monopoly campaign on the box *Sporting Life* 7 May 1994. (The one or ones who give me the hump are the bozos behind Big Mac who wave and grimace at the camera – the sooner he fulfils his threat and lays a few of them out, the better!)

Looking like a hedge dragged through a man backwards.

> *Sunday Express* description of John McCririck, 8 May 1994

We believe it is the first time racing has been covered live from the Middle East.

> Channel 4 Executive Producer ANDREW FRANKLIN on the live coverage of four races from Nad Al Sheba, Dubai on 25 March 1994 (*Racing Post*). Excellent – now tell us why you bothered to inflict such a non-event on us?

Imagine a racing programme that is just that: no zooming off between races for coverage of international badminton tournaments; no boring gaps between races padded out with peripheral guff and, above all, no danger whatsoever of hearing or seeing Eve Pollard.

> ANDREW SIM of *Sporting Life* on Sky TV's *The Winning Post* 27 April 1994

Ninety-four per cent of Channel 4 viewers think that John McCririck's hand-wavings are a load of bollocks.

> Comedienne JO BRAND to Big Mac on BBC 2's science quiz show *Brain Drain* August 1993. And the other six per cent?

Why does Julian Wilson have to say 'orf' in the review of a race? Orf is a disease which affects sheep.

> Letter to the racing press from PETER WILSON, no relation, we presume, of Cumbria, August 1993

Perhaps it ought to be renamed The Moaning Line.

> *Daily Star* TV critic DAVID WOODS on Channel 4's racing bulletin, 21 May 1994

We have to constantly remind our paddock commentators not to say that a horse has a wind problem. That may be a racing term to describe breathing difficulties but the public, of course, does not readily make the association.

> *Channel 4 Racing* producer ANDREW FRANKLIN *The Times* 28 May 1994

I'm convinced the cove who does the racing commentary is going to have a cardiac arrest on air one of these days.

> Warning to BBC Radio's Peter Bromley from creative advertising executive MARK WNEK of Euro RSGC *Campaign* 6 May 1994

Totally irrelevant?

I'm a failure. I can't do anything of any use to anyone. At least if I made nuts and bolts for a car I'd be useful. But I'm totally irrelevant.

> Self-assessment by JOHN McCRIRICK with which many would agree and a few, myself included, would disagree *Daily Star* 13 May 1994

A sexist paddock pillock with all the charm of an armpit.

> Description of JOHN McCRIRICK at his own admission, made by 'a woman journo' *Daily Star* 13 May 1994

He reckons he's a sexual athlete. But the bejewelled, arm-waving John McCririck looks more like a beached whale than a good bet between the sheets.

> CAROLE MALONE finding the charms of Big Mac thoroughly resistible *Daily Star* 13 May 1994

No one's good enough to grill McCririck – he's like a snake, he's better left alone.

> Heavyweight political interviewer BRIAN WALDEN on Channel 4's *Morning Line* 14 May 1994

People like McCririck are blind. They've never sat on a horse in their life. They wouldn't know a horse if it kicked them.

> Trainer CHARLIE BROOKS on John McCririck, talking on BBC Radio 5, reported by Patrick Collins *Mail on Sunday* 20 March 1994

A sexist paddock pillock with all the charm of an armpit

You hear yourself saying 'this should be a really exciting novice hurdle' when you're really thinking 'Christ, and there's another 300 of these ahead'.

> JOHN FRANCOME on the delights of being a racing commentator, to Robert Philip of the *Daily Telegraph* 17 December 1993

If the BBC fails us on this one, I hope that no racing fan will ever pay their TV licence again.

> TIM FITZGEORGE-PARKER on the plans of Channel 4 and Sky to muscle in on BBC's Cheltenham Festival coverage *Raceform Update* 12 February 1994

Jim is brilliant. There's no question that he will take over from me.

> PETER O'SULLEVAN on his appointed heir, 'Aussie' Jim McGrath *The Sun* October 1993

Not just for me, but a recognition of the sport of horseracing.

> PETER O'SULLEVAN on receiving the OBE in the Queen's Birthday Honours List, June 1991

The only exercise I take is a walk to the betting shop.

PETER O'SULLEVAN *Dail Telegraph* 14 March 1994

I have a warmer leaning towards all types of animals than humans and Pat [his wife] said that doubtless I would rather have a horse.

PETER O'SULLEVAN explaining why there were never any O'Sullevans Minor *Daily Telegraph* 14 March 1994

Had he been at Balaclava he would have kept pace with the Charge of the Light Brigade in precise order and described the riders' injuries before they hit the ground.

The Observer sports writer HUGH McILVANNEY on Peter O'Sullevan after the commentator was awarded the OBE in 1977

Sorry, I've had too much Coke, I'm way up . . .

CLARE BALDING during her BBC Radio 5 racing bulletin on 10 October 1993. She later explained, 'I mean I drank too much Coke in the car on the way.'

Given the choice between a vasectomy without an anaesthetic, and listening to Lord Oaksey ramble on about past Whitbread Gold Cups on the *Morning Line* I would make the former a shade of odds on.

MARK WINSTANLEY *Sporting Life* 25 April 1994

In reviewing the race, John said the horse had to dig deeper than Fred West to hold on.

MARK WINSTANLEY on a Francome classic comment *Sporting Life* 12 May 1994

My doctor told me to eat breakfast like a king, lunch like a lord and dinner like a pauper. And I'm still allowed to drink whisky in the evenings.

Racecourse commentator RALEIGH GILBERT on how he shed nearly four stone from his 15st 6lb bulk *Sporting Life* 21 February 1994

It seems to be the reporters who know best and hype up the horses . . . They start writing up horses as world-beaters just because they have seen them finish in front in a gallop. But I can tell you that it is difficult enough for trainers to interpret home gallops.

LUCA CUMANI on work-watchers and writers in April 1991 after his much-vaunted Classic hope Suomi was beaten at Sandown *Daily Telegraph Flat Racing Yearbook* 1992

The press built me up to be a superstar then the next day said I'm the bad boy of racing.

> ADRIAN MAGUIRE, smarting from criticism of his controversial ride on Ramstar and subsequent whip ban *Sporting Life* 28 January 1994

I am more hurt by the press I got from Warwick than I am about the six days' ban.

> ADRIAN MAGUIRE, as above

The press are mainly responsible for making a mountain out of a molehill as regards the whip situation. In the last few years they have lost all their respectability as they continue to ruin the lives of individuals, while making unnecessary problems for racing.

> Former Malton trainer in Bahrain PAT ROHAN *Under Orders* April 1994

The press only want to talk about doom and gloom.

> Occasionally reluctant communicator JENNY PITMAN *Daily Mail* October 1993

If I could get hold of the bastard responsible for the pagination I would be doing the world an immeasurable favour.

> Marketing Director NIGEL MORRIS discussing the difficulties of locating the form in the *Sporting Life* in a review of the racing press in the advertising weekly *Campaign* 18 March 1994

A feat of origamic dexterity.

> As above, discussing the difficulties of turning the pages of the *Life* in outdoor conditions

The coverage is superb, it's well written and it has real authority.

> Final approval of the product from NIGEL MORRIS

Peter Scott, 'Hotspur' in the *Daily Telegraph* for 25 years, died suddenly in April 1994, aged 64 . . . He might not have coined the phrase 'the junkies' jamboree' but it sums up his views.

> GEORGE ENNOR on Peter Scott's opinion of the Breeders' Cup meeting *Racing Post* 6 April 1994

I fancy this one rather strongly.

> *Daily Telegraph* obituary recalling a Scott wager of 50p

Mr Craven A.

Description of Julian Wilson by *The Punter* fanzine, January 1994

The toys soon fly out of their prams at the first sign of flak.

SIMON HOLT on trainers' reaction to criticism by the media *Sporting Life* 24 January 1994

Trainers. . . appear increasingly out of touch with reality, determined to fight for their narrow interests at the expense of the general good of racing.

MARK POPHAM *Weekender* 22 January 1994

Almost my favourite television programme is *The Clothes Show*. I never miss it.

I did not change my newspaper, have not switched TV channels, am still happily with my wife Pat after 42 years marriage and still have the same tailor.

> The loyal PETER O'SULLEVAN reflecting that he was with the *Daily Express* for 36 years, gave his first BBC commentary in 1946 and married 42 years ago

I love to shop. Women's clothes, too. Pat does not come shopping with me but I go with her. Almost my favourite television programme is *The Clothes Show*. I never miss it.

> PETER O'SULLEVAN who bought his first suit from Savile Row firm J. B. Johnstone for £14 14s 0d in 1940 and his latest from the same tailor in 1994 at a 'cost well in excess of four figures' *Sunday Express Magazine* 3 April 1994

I'm the world's worst dresser, so I could do with all of it.

> Envious CLARE BALDING waiting to present her racing bulletin on Radio 5 Live and looking longingly at memorabilia for a Barbra Streisand concert being discussed by host of the show John Inverdale and a guest, 20 April 1994

Going Behind appears to have been recorded in the punishment block of a Grade A prison.

> GREG WOOD on the monthly racing video *The Independent* 21 April 1994

My experience of watching early editions was that I felt as if I'd *been* in prison after sitting through them.

The tone of this show is sometimes painfully chummy and it seems to have been filmed in someone's garage on a budget of £35 including expenses.

> Another uncomplimentary review, this time for Channel 4's *Morning Line* by GILES SMITH *Independent on Sunday* April 1994

It's my first real cock-up and it just goes to show I'm only human.

> BBC radio commentator PETER BROMLEY, having called home the wrong Cesarewitch winner 1993

RACECOURSES

Sheer excitement

We lose one or two customers each year. It's the sheer excitement that the racing brings to everyone. They die of a combination of factors. But everyone's adrenalin and pulse rises at the moments of high drama at Cheltenham and I'm not surprised one or two keel over.

> LORD VESTEY, Chairman of Cheltenham, on the Festival's fatal attraction
> *Sporting Life* 9 March 1994

We're not looking to get more people racing here during the Festival. In 1989 we had 63,000 on Gold Cup day, and that was too many.

> EDWARD GILLESPIE *Pacemaker & Thoroughbred Breeder* March 1994

The best country race meeting in the world.

> Veteran trainer KEN OLIVER on Kelso racecourse *Racing Post*
> 5 February 1994

When we asked if they were looking for bombs, they said no, they were checking to see if we were bringing in food, as this was forbidden.

> *Sporting Life* letter from DAVID DEANE, recalling a bag search at Sandown
> Park, 9 December 1993

Edinburgh is a wretched excuse for a racecourse and how they can charge people to go through the front gates, considering the lack of facilities for the public, will remain one of the great magic tricks of our time.

> J.A. McGRATH *Daily Telegraph* 5 December 1993. Bet he didn't pay to get in.

We have the first Indian franchise on a British racecourse.

> RICHARD MUDDLE on the culinary delights of the new Wolverhampton,
> 6 December 1993

Stunning geometry and its pure, simple and disciplined design.

>Reasons cited for the Queen's Stand at Epsom winning the *Financial Times* architecture award for 1993. Yes – but can you see the horses?

Somebody even tried to get in by flashing an MFI furniture shop receipt.

>Ayr's IVAN STRAKER explaining why abuse of the system led the course to drop cut-price admission for the unemployed. But were people paying for their furniture with Ayr admission tickets?

I'd say my chances of getting the racecourses are only about one in ten.

>Owner and publisher DAVID SULLIVAN on buying Epsom, Sandown and Kempton (*The Guardian* 14 December 1993). One in a million might have been a more accurate guess!

Events at Tir Prince Welsh trotting track recently brought the TV company a BAFTA award for best actuality coverage. We finished in front of the five nations rugby and the Eisteddfod!

> Tir Prince owner BILLY WILLIAMS *Sporting Life* 13 January 1994

I . . . found the press room the crummiest, nastiest, farthest-removed-from-the-action press room in the land.

> CLEMENT FREUD on the delights of Warwick *Sporting Life* 11 January 1994

'Never let me in here again' and 'Too many races'.

> Comments posted in the suggestion box at Warwick, reported by course manager P. McNEILLE. Surely they weren't signed 'C. Freud'? *Sporting Life* 12 January 1994

I loathe it with a passion. All those people who wouldn't know which end bites trying to get spotted by Judith Chalmers, while you're trying to get the saddle down to the horse.

> Trainer CHARLES O'BRIEN on Royal Ascot *The Independent* 3 February 1994

They should close

The bigger courses like Ascot, Goodwood, Sandown, Kempton and Newmarket should have all-weather racing. These courses would benefit from being used more and it would provide more opportunities for owners. . . Racing is trying to subsidise too many racecourses. Some of the smaller courses have bad facilities and if they cannot survive on their own they should close. There isn't enough money to support all 59 courses.

> SHEIKH HAMDAN AL MAKTOUM *Racing Post* 1 June 1994

There are three racecourses beginning with the letter F – namely Fontwell, Folkestone and effing Plumpton.

> Comment attributed to Fred Winter by SIMON HOLT *Sporting Life* 31 January 1994

Why don't racecourses link up together and share the services and costs of keeping a couple of retired racehorses which could be transported from track to track and ridden over the course the day before, and the morning of, racing?

> Suggestion, by fanzine *The Punter*, to improve official going reports, January 1994

In racing there are too many enclosures, too many places where you need a special permit or the right coloured pass. It can't go on. It doesn't make sense.

> MICHAEL CAULFIELD, Jockeys Association *Daily Telegraph* 12 February 1994

Racing is rare among spectator sports in that the spectator often happily pays to watch something he will not be able to see. At some courses, such as Aintree, the action extends so far into the distance that it is invisible even through binoculars.

> SUE MONTGOMERY *IoS* 3 April 1994

I've been on the waiting list for a private box for 20 years and I expect I'll have to wait another 20. You have to pay a bribe to get a seat in the restaurant, and the owners' box is like a two-star hotel.

> Soft porn newspaper magnate DAVID SULLIVAN, after his filly Risky won at Royal Ascot, 1993

Racing does not make money . . . it's the subsidiary things like the caravan sites and golf courses that keep us going.

> DAVID PARMLEY, Managing Director of cash-strapped Newcastle, July 1993

At Aintree a £20 badge entitled you to stand in the torrential rain on the roof of the County Stand – for those who haven't been, an altitude of at least 100 feet is required at Aintree in order to see any of the racing beyond the last two fences. If you asked the people who run Aintree why the County Stand roof hasn't got a roof of its own to protect racegoers I expect you'd get a blank stare and an answer along the lines of 'Sorry, we don't stand there'.

Trying to seek sanctuary . . . in the more modern Queen Mother Stand proved just as frustrating. Any attempt to scale the upper floors offered glimpses of vast spaces sealed off by commissionaires.

And gradually you became aware of the high percentage of the stand which was set aside for hospitality boxes, private luncheon-rooms, Jockey Club members and others who could afford to indulge their deep-rooted desire not to mingle with the public.

Newmarket's Rowley Course already has a head start in the Barmy Design Stakes, since the track itself is mostly beyond the clear sight of racegoers, with only the last two furlongs offering a coherent view. But the stands compound the insult to the intelligence and the wallet by being littered with signs reading 'No admission', 'Private', 'Jockey Club Only'. The average customer is made to feel like an intruder upon a private estate.

Newbury's new Berkshire Stand is, at least, a striking and innovative building. The public spaces are well appointed and the catering and viewing facilities are well above the usual standard... But even in this welcome exception to the rule there seemed to be a disproportionate provision of private boxes and lunching suites. I wonder if these facilities really do bring in sufficient money to justify their existence or whether they're simply the product of a kind of reflex homage to a class system based on privacy and exclusion.

> Thought-provoking description of STAN HEY's trips to three racecourses *Independent on Sunday* 24 April 1994. 'Privilege', 'Privacy', 'Intruder'. Surely some mistake?

Ally Pally was really rather an awful racecourse from every point of view.

> Down-to-earth assessment of what is now remembered as being an atmospheric, sadly missed London track – Alexandra Park which shut in 1970 – by ROGER MORTIMER, 1979

Recent improvements

Despite recent improvements, and the unique race-day atmosphere, Aintree will never be a favourite of mine. A flat, bleak, ugly place; the Mildmay course unappealing, the National course infinitely more majestic when seen from your living room.

> Description unlikely to find a place in the Tourist Guide to Liverpool, of Aintree, by DAVID ASHFORTH *Sporting Life* 9 April 1994

I attended Brighton races in foul weather and I was in need of sustenance. For the first time I came upon a gourmet curry wagon. The quality and taste were absolutely superb and stood out among the mediocre and dreary fare usually offered to racegoers.

> KEITH WRIGHT, Bournemouth, letter to *Racing Post* 19 April 1994

The Northern Ireland course has been having problem with rabbit holes and it has not been possible to use the chase circuit since January.

> *Sporting Life* story on Down Royal (16 April 1994), where they obviously should have used rather more of the old bunny

I want Newmarket to be voted Racecourse of the Year for the next three years. I have started by talking to all the men, every lavatory attendant, and told them I want to make our customers happy.

> Brough Scott reporting the comments of Newmarket Chairman PETER PLAYER who is obviously aiming at a new, higher bog standard service at racing's HQ *Racing Post* 5 May 1994

Newmarket is full of statues of naked horses but there's not one of Mistress Gwyn and her famous charms. It would jolly things up.

> BROUGH SCOTT calling for due recognition of the mistress of Charles II, who first promoted racing at Newmarket *Racing Post* 5 May 1994

We were told the Sefton Course would have to be closed for a while to encourage a healthier coverage of grass. As that announcement was made in the late sixties we must assume it is growing very slowly.

> IAN CARNABY on Newmarket's mysterious non-sprouting turf *Sporting Life* 5 May 1994

It costs £2000 a day just to run the nine escalators in the grandstand.

> Not many people know that – but Newmarket Clerk of the Course NICK LEES does *Bulletin for Racing and Breeding* April 1994

My suggestion is that we do away with the National Stud and build a new all-weather and grass track on the site, along the lines of Southwell. Given the extra space, a grass jumping track might be possible too. We already have plenty of car-parking space available, and direct access from the A45 would be a great idea. The site would be fully utilised – we could have floodlit racing all year.

> Trainer MARK TOMPKINS' remarkable plan to revolutionise Newmarket in a letter to the *Sporting Life*. Do we detect just the teeniest trace of sarcasm directed at those looking to 'update' the course? *Sporting Life* 11 May 1994

It is very shortsighted of racecourses to act as if they are doing the owners a favour by admitting them to watch their own horses . . . In what other sport are the players asked to pay to get in?

> Trainer MARK JOHNSTON wondering why trainers and owners do not get automatic complimentary admission to all courses *Sporting Life* 14 May 1994

Every stall at Punchestown sells fruit and chocolate. For some reason there is a presumption at Irish race meetings that no sane person would want to go home without first equipping him or herself with 'four Mars bars for £1 and a large bag of pears'. At Punchestown this view is taken to its extreme.

> A choc-full PAUL HAIGH, who has in his time been accused of being every type of fruit and nut case, at the Punchestown Festival *Sunday Telegraph* 1 May 1994

A racecourse should be a place where you would be happy – if that's the right word – to have a heart attack.

> (And many probably feel that they're about to when they back a winner only for a stewards' inquiry to be called!) Jockey Club medical adviser DR MICHAEL TURNER on the need for top medical facilities to be available at all courses *Racing Post* 19 May 1994

The simple truth is that some of our racecourses are poorly run and unimaginatively managed and couldn't attract extra customers if Arkle, Desert Orchid, Nijinsky and the Archangel Gabriel all appeared on the same card.

> *Sporting Life* 18 May 1994. Who would you make favourite of those runners?

It certainly enjoys in a peculiar manner royal patronage, and our aristocracy flock to it pretty much as they did a quarter of a century ago; but it has long lost all claims to exclusiveness, and with them have gone much that no doubt rendered Ascot the pleasantest of race meetings. It is a huge metropolitan gathering, retaining indeed some of the old prestige in the scarlet liveries of the Royal party and the select circle in the Royal Enclosure, but in all other respects an Ascot of the people.

> *The Times* in an 1866 editorial complaining about the 'vulgarisation' of Royal Ascot

What Brighton has done amounts to highway robbery. The track was unraceable, but they went ahead with one race and then pocketed people's money. No apology was made, and it's the most disgraceful thing I have ever seen.

> Bookmaker JOE BATES after a meeting at Brighton was abandoned following the first race because heavy rain had turned the track into a mudbath. But because one race had been run no refund was offered to racegoers *The Sun* 27 May 1994

A gong sounded at the start of every race to stop people betting. Sometimes some of the bookies opposite the stand – now a car park – who had lost could be seen running away before the last race, throwing down their satchels as they went, with the punters in hot pursuit.

> Memories of Goodwood, by probably the course's longest 'serving' spectator and racegoer, GERALD LE BLOUNT KIDD, who first visited the course in 1914, aged four *Goodwood 1994 Racecourse Annual*

I heard a man

It rubs salt into the wound when I see the Worcester rowing eight going down the course and screaming 'photograph' as they pass the winning post!

> Worcester General Manager JACK BENNETT, surveying his course, flooded by the River Severn *The Independent* 6 January 1994

I've not found racecourses to be prejudiced, although people often take a second look.

> Black Jamaican HOWARD GROVES, front man for the Metropolitan Police Racing Club, owners of Walk The Beat. He's a Detective Sergeant *Sunday Express* 13 February 1994

I heard a man in the lavatory queue say to his friend: 'Yes, I know there are inconveniences but at least you can be sure the IRA won't bomb the place.'

PETER CORRIGAN on the Cheltenham Festival *Independent on Sunday* 20 March 1994

Tap-dancing, acting and directing in the theatre, juggling . . . all are hobbies of Edward Gillespie, Manager of Cheltenham race-course.

PETER SCUDAMORE *Daily Mail* 13 January 1994

We have cameras at 59 courses. Twice between races they inadvertently filmed intimate activity of a strictly non-racing variety.

Anonymous SIS spokesman *The Sun* 5 February 1994

It was a very different cup of tea then; people were coming with really scruffy jeans, jeans with holes in them, in a filthy state. Nowadays they are nicely dressed in smart jeans like you or I might wear.

Ascot Clerk of the Course NICHOLAS BEAUMONT (he wears jeans?) explaining why the course had lifted its ban on denims and jeans in its Tattersalls enclosure, imposed in January 1990 *Racing Post* October 1993

Quite ridiculous

I'm delighted that at last they've come to realise that jeans are not a prohibited substance. It was quite ridiculous; they seem to think they can do whatever they like with regard to the people who pay.

I don't think the Queen would be too offended to see someone leaning over the rails wearing jeans.

> Racegoers Club representative REG GRIFFIN, welcoming Ascot's relaxation of the jeans ban and calling for it to be extended to the Royal Meeting

I wanted my name in the form book.

> Librarian AUDREY BUTTERY who celebrated her retirement after 44 years by sponsoring a race named after her at Market Rasen in September 1993

It is deeply regretted by all that Ascot should be visited this year by the Prince of Wales, and the Queen has done all she can to prevent it, but in vain. It is not because the Queen thinks races the dullest things in the world that she is so anxious that the Prince of Wales should discountenance them as much as possible but on account of the horrible gambling, the ruin to hundreds of families and the heart-break of parents caused thereby, which lowers the higher classes frightfully.

> No, not a recent communication by QE II about Prince Charles, in fact an extract from a letter written in 1872 by QUEEN VICTORIA, in the third person, to one of the royal tutors

We've made it as easy as possible for people to get a drink – but we've got to enable them to get rid of it too.

> EDWARD GILLESPIE on the Cheltenham Festival *Racing Post* 19 March 1994

There is one particular person who has come here to die today. He knows he is dying and he just hopes it happens today. But he won't die here. We'll make sure he gets away.

> Cheltenham Manager EDWARD GILLESPIE, Gold Cup Day 1994

This is my 28th Cheltenham. A friend of mine once lost all his money at cards on the boat over and had to turn back for home without setting foot in England.

> Irish visitor to Cheltenham, FATHER SEAN BREEN *The Guardian* 18 March 1994

This is really one of those buildings where the best view is from in it, senses preferably anaesthetised by a stiff drink.

A clumpy, Frankensteinian agglomeration of pitched roofs, folksy dormers and faux Victorian conservatories that appear to have suffered a near fatal attack of Supermarket Vernacular. An overblown confection resembling a mutant cricket pavilion.

Like the punters it attracts, racecourse architecture is usually a bit rough and ready.

> CATHERINE SLESSOR on Newbury's £10 million Berkshire Grandstand in the *Architectural Review* March 1994

Don't bore me with Wordsworth's ridiculous daffodils. The sublime spectacle of encroaching spring is Cheltenham Racecourse and a host of golden bookies swaying between Red Alert and Blue Funk.

> The *Daily Mail*'s IAN WOOLDRIDGE prior to the 1991 Festival

The Queen Alexandra Stakes

There was controversy in December 1993 when Ascot decided to change the distance of the historic Queen Alexandra Stakes:

It was being won by not particularly good hurdlers.

> Ascot Clerk of the Course NICKY BEAUMONT, announcing the 129-year-old Queen Alexandra Stakes was to be cut from $2^3/_4$ miles to a 10-furlong handicap

These people are destroying the tradition of racing. There is a sickness at Ascot that needs to be cured.

> JOHN McCRIRICK's reaction on *Morning Line* 11 December 1993 to the announcement

When I go out to lunch I feel naked without a form.

> PETER O'SULLEVAN, supporting the petition organised by John Livingstone-Learmonth to reprieve the Queen Alexandra States *Sporting Life* 6 January 1994

It is as much of a sacrilege as if they did away with Trooping the Colour.

> JIMMY LINDLEY *Sporting Life* 6 January 1994

We have had about six letters against the change and one for.

Ascot Clerk of the Course NICKY BEAUMONT, on public response to the change *Racing Post* 6 January 1994

If the Queen Alexandra should continue as it is just because that is the way it has always been, we might as well go back to tape starts in Flat races and jockeys wearing spurs.

GREG WOOD *The Independent* 10 January 1994

We're prostituting the whole game – it is getting more like dog racing every day. We are giving in to commercialism.

DAVID ELSWORTH *Sporting Life* 7 January 1994

It is inexcusable to stand fast on having no sponsorship.

DAVID HOOD of William Hill after Ascot authorities rejected his firm's bid to save the Queen Alexandra by sponsoring a 10-furlong handicap to be run alongside it on the same Royal Ascot card *Sporting Life* 12 January 1994

The Ascot Trustees have decided that the conditions and distance of the race will remain unaltered for 1994.

Ascot's cave-in *Sporting Life* 13 January 1994

I am very pleased that Ascot have reacted so quickly.

Petition organiser and modest hero of the campaign, JOHN LIVINGSTONE-LEARMONTH *Racing Post* 13 January 1994

THE HORSES

The best I'll ever train

Carvills Hill is the best I'll ever train.

> Trainer MARTIN PIPE *Sporting Life* October 1993

Carvills Hill had a fantastic engine but there was a flaw in his chassis and suspension.

> Carvills Hill's first trainer, JIM DREAPER, on the horse's retirement *Sporting Life* 1 March 1994

He's the best horse I've ever trained.

> ANDRE FABRE after Zafonic won the 1993 2000 Guineas

The Dikler was one of the most beautiful jumping horses I have ever seen in my life.

> The HON. NICHOLAS SOAMES, MP *Horse and Hound* 12 May 1994

He's a slightly neurotic twit.

> ROSEMARY HENDERSON on Fiddlers Pike on whom the 51-year-old finished fifth in the 1994 Grand National *Mail on Sunday* 10 April 1994

It's like making love every time I get on the horse.

> WILLIE CARSON paying the ultimate compliment to Derby winner Nashwan in 1989

King kicks, bites and tramples the hell out of me, but with Robert he's as gentle as a lamb.

> King Credo's trainer STEVE WOODMAN on the relationship between the horse and his great fan, five-year-old handicapped lad Robert Byrne *Daily Star* 23 November 1993

He kicked me as I was brushing him down, and splattered my nose across my face. I reset it myself as I didn't have time to go to hospital. You'd think I'd hate him, but I love the horse.

> Trainer NORMAN BABBAGE on his 50/1 Worcester winner Barely Black, 8 December 1993

Last year The Fellow would have cost us millions, and now he has saved us fortunes. What a beautiful horse!

> ROB HARTNETT of Coral after The Fellow's 1994 Cheltenham Gold Cup victory *Sporting Life* 18 March 1994

I guarantee you The Fellow has a bigger, more faithful following in Britain than he does here.

> French-based former jockey GUY LANDAU *Racing Post* 8 April 1994

Snurge made us all swallow our sneers, bringing nothing but glory to his owner's unglamorous schoolboy nickname.

> JOHN OAKSEY *Daily Telegraph Flat Racing Yearbook* 1992 on the horse who became the top British-trained prize-money winner of all time.

On Arazi

I couldn't believe Arazi was accelerating that fast so easily. I had goose bumps. It was unreal. I thought I was on the next Secretariat. It was the greatest turn of foot I have ever experienced.

PATRICK VALENZUELA after Arazi's stunning 1991 Breeders' Cup Juvenile victory

The greatest performance I've ever seen.

Top US trainer SHUG McGAUGHEY

The best performance I've ever seen from a two-year-old and one of the most amazing performances I've seen in 28 years as a handicapper.

Jockey Club handicapper GEOFFREY GIBBS

What a monster. I saw Swaps and Secretariat run like that, but never from that far back. That was amazing.

Trainer of the runner-up, Bertrand, BRUCE HEADLEY

Superlative, staggering, overwhelming performance.

Daily Telegraph Flat Racing Yearbook 1992, headline

Arazi is not just the best horse I have ever owned – he's the best horse anyone has ever owned.

ALLEN PAULSON in October 1991 after the then wonder two-year-old Arazi had galloped away with a race at Longchamp. Sadly the horse failed to reproduce his form as a three-year-old.

Arazi, unhurried after breaking slowly, angled to the inside after settling suddenly racing into the far turn, came out between horses to continue his run, caught Bertrando with a rush after going six furlongs, drifted out while drawing off into the stretch, increased his advantage under a brisk hand ride inside the final furlong, then was taken in hand through the final 70 yards.

Official Breeders' Cup race description

Breathtaking – literally. Jet-lagged, on dirt for the first time, from a hideous outside stall 14, this equine freak . . . scythed snipe-like through America's best, leaving astonished racegoers drained and gasping for oxygen. The old Kentucky home of the Thoroughbred had never witnessed his like before.

> JOHN McCRIRICK *Channel 4 Racing Companion* 1992, Sidgwick & Jackson

Under-trained and over-ridden.

> New York newspaper comment after Arazi had failed in the 1992 Kentucky Derby

I will remember him... and her

In 17 outings for us Superfluous never, ever beat another horse home – which must be some kind of record. But I will remember him long after I have forgotten more successful animals I have been fortunate enough to part-own.

> Racing journalist COLIN MACKENZIE

I love her to death.

> GEORGE DUFFIELD on User Friendly after they had been narrowly beaten in the 1992 Arc

I've never ridden a better horse.

> CASH ASMUSSEN on Suave Dancer after he won the Prix du Jockey Club, 2 June 1991

This is the best horse that I have ridden.

> CASH ASMUSSEN on Suave Dancer after he won the Arc de Triomphe, 6 October 1991. At least he's consistent!

He is the best I've seen in 30 years in the saddle.

> BRUCE RAYMOND on Generous, July 1991

Halkopous was undoubtedly doped or got at in some way in the Irish Champion Hurdle.

> Trainer MARK TOMPKINS *The Independent* 11 December 1993

He's had more operations than Joan Collins – and maybe more men working on him.

> JENNY PITMAN in 1988 on her injury prone Gold Cup winner Burrough Hill Lad

He's taken loads of chunks out of me over the years. I give him a carrot every night – and he still hates me.

> NICKY HENDERSON in 1987 on his ungrateful triple Champion Hurdler See You Then. Perhaps he was trying to tell Nicky that he was sick of bloody carrots!

I never really know how fit she is. Most days she couldn't even beat a donkey.

> IAN BALDING on Lochsong. Must be some donkey!

It completely poisoned the horse.

> Trainer JOHN PANVERT, claiming his Toughnutocrack was adversely affected by the all-weather surface at Lingfield when last of 12 there on 4 February *Racing Post*

Shergar Is Alive.

> Banner headline in *The Sun* March 1991, revealing that Shergar was alive and well and living in the Channel Islands

It was like going into someone's bedroom a week after they've died. You have just been to the funeral and you come back to look at their empty bedroom. It's a terrible feeling, believe me.

> Part-owner of Shergar, vet STAN COSGROVE, on visiting Shergar's box shortly after the horse had been kidnapped *The Guardian* 18 March 1994

I realised then, when that £80,000 disappeared, that the horse was dead.

> STAN COSGROVE, on handing over £80,000 to a dubious contact whose claims that he knew where Shergar was proved unfounded *The Guardian* 18 March 1994

Shergar was destroyed within hours of being abducted. The body was buried in a bog at Aughnasheelin near Ballinamore.

> Information supplied to Stan Cosgrove by life-serving prisoner with IRA links, SEAN O'CALLAGHAN *The Guardian* 18 March 1994

He must have been stung by a bee.

> An only half-joking JEAN HISLOP, on Roberto, who had just inflicted the first and only defeat of his career on Brigadier Gerard in the 1972 Benson & Hedges Gold Cup at York, in course record time

He was just something else – a truly great horse.

WALTER SWINBURN on Shergar *Weekender* 30 April 1994

Roberto's trouble was that, in equine terms, he was the equivalent of a manic depressive.

CAMILLA POWER reflecting on how Derby winner Roberto, who was also the only horse to defeat Brigadier Gerard, never really received true recognition of his feats *Pacemaker & Thoroughbred Breeder* June 1994

Both sets of experts came to the conclusion that the horse developed a form of travel sickness.

Trainer PADDY PRENDERGAST who had consulted a veterinary college and equine centre for an insight into the reason for his Winter Belle's poor performance when taken from Ireland to race at the Cheltenham Festival *Sporting Life* 30 March 1994

I can honestly say

I can honestly say that I've never seen a horse look more relieved in all my life.

Trainer DAVID NICHOLSON commenting after having his Silver Wisp gelded – is he sure that was a look of relief? *Racing Post* 10 November 1993

He was not only a top-class racehorse, he was also my best mate.

> Trainer PETER CHAPPLE-HYAM following the death of his highly rated three-year-old Stonehatch, rated the second best two-year-old in Britain *Racing Post* 4 April 1994

When the RSPCA saw the scene in Old Gringo in which Twister pretends to be shot in the head, it couldn't believe he'd survived and lobbied to ban the British cinema release of the movie.

> BART MILLS on former Utah racehorse Heaven Above, turned Hollywood stunt-star Twister, whose ability to fall down 'dead' for the movie cameras in dramatic style has earned owner Rudy Ugland £150,000 *Mail on Sunday* 17 April 1994

Bookmakers William Hill offer 200/1 against Nijinsky's last [foal] being first past the post at Epsom in three years. Goodbody [stud manager] is not the only one whose comments suggest that forward-thinking punters snapping up those odds might find themselves participating in the biggest 'steal' since the Great Train Robbery.

> *Sunday Times* racing correspondent JOHN KARTER who is so keen on the 1996 Derby chances of the Nijinsky-It's In The Air foal that he snapped up a tenner's worth at 200–1 – while his then sports editor Chris Nawrat had rather more faith in JK's tipping abilities than I do by placing a more substantial 'monkey' on to win £100,000, 18 July 1993

The horse falls three times in the Grand National two weeks previously; his jockey is told he's mad to take the ride; his trainer hasn't had a winner since January and stays at home to tend the lambs; his owner despairs about the overnight rain and doesn't have a penny on him; result – Ushers Island wins the Whitbread Gold Cup at 25/1.

> CHRIS HAWKINS *The Guardian* 25 April 1994

You couldn't rule out a plague of flies getting racing abandoned where he's due to run.

> Trainer MOUSE MORRIS on his apparently jinxed Cahervillahow who managed to find all the hard luck going (*Racing Post* 27 November 1993). Tragically the horse was later killed.

He pees to his own line and length.

> Trainer TONY HIDE on his two-year-old Backward Point, who was 'born with his genitals back to front' *Racing Post* 29 April 1994

It's one of my biggest regrets that he didn't win the Gold Cup in 1988. I remain convinced that he was interfered with.

DAVID BARONS, announcing his retirement and commenting on one of the best he handled, jumper Playschool *Sporting Life* 7 May 1994

He's a natural in the air, and can nod the ball across to adjoining boxes.

RICHARD HANNON on the heading skills of Right Win, who is so playful at home that his handler suspended footballs from the ceiling of his box to divert his attention. Appropriately enough he was a winner at Newbury on FA Cup Final day! *Sunday Express* 15 April 1994

In grave danger of being reduced to Spam.

Less than complimentary comment by point-to-point 'bible', Mackenzie and Selby, about 10-year-old Spambruco, who silenced the detractors with a 20/1 win at Heythrop's point-to-point in May. *Horse and Hound* 19 May 1994

He is a miracle horse, really, his off-fore turns out at right angles.

Trainer MICHAEL BELL on his Newcastle winner Thick As Thieves *Racing Post* 20 May 1994

The horse is only a little bit bigger than the singer.

Trainer's wife PEGGY COTTRELL after their Montserrat, named after the operatic soprano, had won at Windsor *Sporting Life* 25 May 1994

I suppose Turtle Island's win would have to rate just about top of my Classic winners. For a horse to come from last to first and win a Classic by 15 lengths is quite a feat. It's almost as if you are talking about jumping distances.

ROBERT SANGSTER, no stranger to Classic triumphs, on the Irish 2000 Guineas winner *Racing Post* 21 May 1994

The ideal racehorse

The ideal racehorse has more speed than the best specialist sprinter, although he may never in fact race over a shorter distance than seven furlongs, and is supreme over distances from one to one and three-quarter miles at three years old and upwards.

A definition of the ideal racehorse put forward in 1975 by the Pattern of Racing Committee headed by the Duke of Norfolk

I didn't want any old horse – it had to be Sabin Du Loir. But Sue explained that no other living creature is allowed on the island and, as I'd hate to wish my old friend into an early grave, I opted for some snorkelling equipment instead.

PETER SCUDAMORE being forced to reject one of his former equine pals as his 'luxury' item when he appeared on *Desert Island Discs* presented by Sue Lawley *Sporting Life* 26 May 1994

Avoid a horse with piggy eyes. They tend to be dishonest, like humans who have their eyes close together. A horse with small eyes won't give the race everything it has.

Trainer CHARLIE BROOKS whose own eyes are obviously large and miles apart *Daily Mail* 30 April 1994

TRAINERS

Hours of agony for moments of glory

This game is about hours of agony for moments of glory.

> JOHN HILLS reporting a favourite phrase of his Dad, trainer Barry Hills
> *Sporting Life* 1 June 1994

Everybody imagines he's the most laid-back character. Nothing could be further from the truth. He gets terribly wound up.

> Owner ROBERT SANGSTER on trainer Peter Chapple-Hyam *Daily Express*
> 1 June 1994

Lots of people still can't believe what's going on. They think somebody else must be doing it. It's jealousy and you'll always get that when someone's doing well.

> MICK CHANNON on his great start to the season *Mail on Sunday* 5 June
> 1994

He takes no prisoners before breakfast, and any time before noon is dangerous, but he gets more placid as the day goes on.

> A 'long-serving' lad discussing Barry Hills – obviously a man after my
> own heart – although I'm a bit touchy up to and including midnight, as
> well! *Racing Post* 1 June 1994

I am going back to basics. I aim to get as much as I can in as little time as I can.

> BARNEY CURLEY after Moynsha House won at Fontwell *Daily Star*
> 18 January 1994

Del-boy Trotter meets Valentino.

> MARCUS ARMYTAGE's description of trainer Charlie Mann *Daily Telegraph*
> 12 February 1994

The first thing I trained was a goat.

> SUE BRAMALL *Sporting Life* 19 January 1994

I remember when his XI played against his stable lads. We were 36 for 5 when he marched to the wicket, waving his bat, and told me at the other end: 'Okay, let's stop the rot.' Sadly, he was bowled first ball by a full toss.

> JULIAN WILSON recalling a classic Michael Stoute innings *The Sun* 4 June 1994

If he wins I shall syndicate him for stud next season.

> SUE SCARGILL, wife of trainer Dr Jon Scargill, on his decision to compete in the 1994 London Marathon *Sporting Life*

The boss [his Dad, Vincent] trained 40 Classic winners and more than 20 Cheltenham winners. If I was worried about trying to match that I'd soon end up in a lunatic asylum.

> Trainer CHARLES O'BRIEN *The Independent* 3 February 1994

Sense of humour

If you didn't have a sense of humour you'd go mad in this game. Happy people get happy horses.

> 1993 champion trainer RICHARD HANNON *Daily Express* 9 November 1993

There are plenty of different ways to get a horse fit. But the real secret is in keeping the horse happy.

> Triple Melbourne Cup-winning trainer GEORGE HANLON *Sunday Telegraph* October 1993

The self-appointed God of racing.

> DAVID NICHOLSON's considered opinion of *Sporting Life* writer Geoff Lester, who had dared to be critical of Adrian Maguire's riding *Sporting Life* 18 January 1994

Francome was on a cert, but came from miles back. He never rode for me again.

> NEVILLE CALLAGHAN, reflecting on the ride John Francome gave his 1982 Triumph Hurdle favourite Royal Vulcan *The Sun* October 1993

Mount Athos would have to have a nose like Pinnocchio on his worst behaviour to have any chance of sharing first place.

> Trainer CHARLIE MANN, a little aggrieved that his Fifth Amendment was ruled to have dead-heated with Mount Athos, whose nose was obscured in the official photograph, at Uttoxeter. It was, of course, purely coincidental that Mount Athos was owned by Hilda Clarke, wife of racecourse chairman Stan, after whom the race was named *Sporting Life* 15 February 1994

It seems to me that one minute the Jockey Club wants jockeys to try harder and the next not to try too hard.

> MARTIN PIPE, reflecting on the whip controversy *Sporting Life* 1 January 1994

It can be very hard to get through to jockeys. Some are deaf, some can't count and some are brilliant.

> MARTIN PIPE *Sporting Life* 1 January 1994

If I've got a runner I fancy I usually go and sit in the toilet.

> Trainer PADDY BUTLER *Sunday Times* 16 January 1994

A half-hearted trainer.

> Mocking self-description by trainer CHARLIE MOORE who had a multiple by-pass operation after three heart attacks *The Guardian* 15 January 1994

It is not about being able to fight. It is more about health and fitness.

> Trainer TIM ETHERINGTON on his martial arts speciality Wing Chun *Daily Telegraph* February 1994

Old is the son of a tailor. The paradox is that he short-heads Nigel Twiston-Davies for the illustrious position of worst-dressed trainer.

> MARCUS ARMYTAGE on Jim Old *Daily Telegraph* 5 March 1994

Maybe I would attract more owners if I was better on the bullshit.

> Trainer DAVID ELSWORTH *Sporting Life* 15 March 1994

I'll tell the owners of the Italian job that I will be in Germany and vice versa to the others. Meanwhile, I will be sitting at home having a bit of roast beef.

> Champion trainer RICHARD HANNON, who had weekend runners in Italy and Germany and was asked where he would go *The Times* 6 November 1993

There's many a week when our pensions have gone towards paying the wages.

> 70-year-old ALF SMITH, the only trainer left in Beverly (*Racing Post* October 1993). His wife Elma is five years his junior.

We have Radio One playing in every box – it keeps the horses relaxed.

> Champion jumps trainer MARTIN PIPE *Sporting Life* November 1993

Lester Piggott's a wonderful jockey, I agree. But, like some Flat race jockeys, he has exploited racing. He's a taker, not a giver.

> Trainer DAVID ELSWORTH reported in *Mail on Sunday* by Ivor Herbert, August 1993

Sometimes I can see them thinking, 'He's just a waste disposal bloke from London – what does he know?'

> Cockney trainer TERRY MILLS on the jockeys who ride for him

I am having a good year, but there is no point in waiting until I have a bad one before advertising. It'll be too late then.

> BEN HANBURY, who spent £20,000 in 1993 advertising his facilities worldwide

I hate mediocre people. I just don't take the time to talk to them.

> ANDRE FABRE. No, I've never spoken to him!

I'm going to carry on until I'm 96, then I might have four years' retirement.

> JENNY PITMAN

As a cyclist I had to know how to keep in shape and, basically, the theory is much the same with horses.

> Jump trainer JOHN HELLENS, (*Raceform Update* October 1993), who must be used to hearing 'on yer bike'!

It's rather like being asked to describe a pretty girl. One man can look at a horse and like it very much, but another may not be able to stand the sight of it.

> PETER WALWYN

Kenneth has only two gears – fast asleep or flat out.

HARRY BEEBY on veteran trainer Ken Oliver who had just celebrated his 80th birthday *Under Orders* April 1994

Win or lose, we'll have a booze.

Slogan attributed to KEN 'Benign Bishop' OLIVER, the veteran trainer, by the *Daily Telegraph* 2 March 1993

I may retire and go to stud myself after this!

Trainer RICHARD PRICE after his Flakey Dove won the 1994 Champion Hurdle *Racing Post* 16 March 1994

Ride him with balls of steel.

Advice from trainer EDWARD O'GRADY to jockey Charlie Swan before the latter rode 11/1 Cheltenham Festival winner Time For A Run *Sporting Life* 17 March 1994

You can treat crooks and thieves like that, but not me.

JOHN UPSON on the decision by owner Andrew Cohen to remove his 19 horses from the yard *Sporting Life* 7 March 1994

He has an accent that causes cultivated Home Counties voices to ask if they are listening to Urdu.

The Times' Irish racing correspondent, 8 March 1994, on Irish trainer TOM FOLEY

I don't like ties. I get dizzy. I feel confined and I never put one on unless I absolutely have to.

Irish trainer TOM FOLEY, said never to have worn a tie at a racecourse (*The Times* 8 March 1994). He broke his rule, however, when his Danoli won at the Cheltenham Festival in 1994.

Talk's cheap, it's money that buys horses.

MICK CHANNON *Sporting Life* 21 March 1993

Trainer John White, at the time convinced that his horse had been nobbled, subsequently blamed his coltish, over-sexed temperament.

TIM FITZGEORGE-PARKER explaining that there just might be reasons other than being 'got at' to explain why horses sometimes perform below their best *Raceform Update* October 1993

You hear trainers saying, 'If only he had jumped the last he would have won.' This reminds me of the saying that if your aunt had balls she would be your uncle.

> NIGEL TWISTON-DAVIES, Horse Race Writers Association Luncheon, December 1993

I am a fat, scruffy trainer with superb facilities who gets the horses fit and has smashing staff.

> Self-description by NIGEL TWISTON-DAVIES at the 1993 Horse Race Writers Association lunch

I'm not a jockey groupie really and I reckon a lot of the praise and accolades they get is too much.

> DAVID ELSWORTH, September 1993

About bloody time.

> Trainer NORMAN MACAULEY welcoming Join The Clan in late June 1993 at Doncaster, his first turf winner of the year

A complete and utter waste of money.

> BARNEY CURLEY'S considered view of the BHB *The Independent* 13 December 1993

If there was an exam on racing, 95 per cent of them would fail.

> BARNEY CURLEY 'on fellow trainers and the racing press', quoted by John Cobb *The Independent* 13 December 1993

Not my style

I'm not a good loser. I'm conscious of the fact that I ought to be more gracious in defeat. I should rush up and congratulate the winning trainer more than I do, but I can't put on an act because that's not my style. It's not resentment, I just prefer winning myself.

> HENRY CECIL on losing *Sporting Life* 23 March 1994

Ron, if you get a new owner, don't win a race for two years. Get them used to losing first!

> Advice to trainer Ron Hodges, from former jockey and permit holder JOHN GAMBLE

I'm not a good loser

It will take a very, very good man to catch me. Plenty have tried, but I'm only in love with my horses at present.

> 30-year-old trainer GAY KELLEWAY *The Sun* 26 March 1994

The most difficult decision I have had to make in racing.

> Trainer RICHARD PRICE whose Flakey Dove was ridden by Mark Dwyer to win the Champion Hurdle, only for Dwyer to be 'jocked off' in favour of Richard Dunwoody next time out (*Racing Post* 30 March 1994). What 'price' loyalty?

I never talked to the press. I had to get my living off the bookmakers.

> Trainer SNOWY PARKER who died in March 1994 aged 90, reported by racing writer Richard Onslow *Sporting Life* 30 March 1994

I'd like to see all water jumps filled in. They are wretched obstacles that serve no purpose – all they do is trap horses into making mistakes.

> Trainer OWEN BRENNAN – not one of racing's wets, obviously *Racing Post* 31 March 1994

I've had the greatest romances in my life with my horses.

> JENNY PITMAN, BBC TV, 9 April 1994

One of the greatest training feats I have ever seen in my life.

> Veteran handler FULKE WALWYN on the achievement of Stow on the Wold trainer Jane Pilkington, whose Willie Wumpkins won the Coral Golden Hurdle at Cheltenham for the third consecutive year in March 1981

Like the Manchester United manager, Alex Ferguson, the champion trainer has unwisely taken on a fortress mentality, treating anyone from outside with suspicion. He believes everyone would like to see him fail, a paranoia which is one certain way to get popular opinion against you.

> RICHARD EDMONDSON on Martin Pipe *The Independent* 11 April 1994

When I started, horses had begun to go in their coats by the time you got to York in August. Now they're all still shining at the Ebor meeting as though it's the middle of summer.

> RICHARD HANNON, quoted by Paul Haigh (*Racing Post* 19 April 1994), on how much later in the year horses now seem to be 'blooming' since the days when he began training less than a quarter of a century ago

I'm now only 43 Classic winners behind Vincent.

> Former assistant to Vincent O'Brien, MICHAEL KAUNTZE, whose Kooyonga had just won the Irish 1000 Guineas, 25 May 1991

If I'd been running around all my life with an inflamed testicle and it was suddenly sorted out I'm sure I'd run faster.

> The same MICHAEL KAUNTZE, this time explaining Selkirk's improved form in winning Ascot's Queen Elizabeth II Stakes at 10/1 three weeks after an operation to remove a testicle, 28 September 1991

I have spent more time feeling Delius's front legs than my wife Carol's!

> RICHARD LEE after his injury-prone Delius made a winning comeback at Kempton *Sporting Life* January 1988

It's tragic. It has ruined the race – even for me.

> DAVID NICHOLSON, whose Charter Party had just won the Cheltenham Gold Cup, after learning that 1985 winner Forgive 'N' Forget had been killed in the same race *Sporting Life* March 1988.

He can fall down and still win.

> Declared by the course commentator as the Terry Biddlecombe mount
> Dark Jet came to the last at Sandown, where he promptly fell, slithered
> along the ground on his belly, got back on his feet and went on to win
> *Sporting Life* 13 December 1968

I have had over 100 horses with him, and though he is a bizarre character and is always blaming jockeys, I have enjoyed Group One success and made money.

> Owner DAVID SULLIVAN on trainer Paul Kelleway *Sporting Life* October
> 1993

You've got to get them mentally as well as physically fit.

> MARK PITMAN *Daily Mail* October 1993

I want to teach Mark things about training he ain't going to read in a book. I want him to recognise leg problems before they become injuries. Any fool can get a horse fit – I want to teach him when the peach is ripe to pluck it. I want him to be the best.

> JENNY PITMAN, preparing to knock her son and new assistant, Mark, into
> shape *Daily Mail* October 1993

When I go racing it is to work. I don't have the time to say hello.

> French trainer ANDRE FABRE *Sporting Life* November 1993

It is a competitive profession in every way. If you want to succeed in life you need to take things from other people.

> ANDRE FABRE *Sporting Life* November 1993

I used to think jockeys were only as good as the horses they rode, but Frankie is something special.

> Trainer DAVID CHAPMAN, for whom Frankie Dettori had just ridden a 35/1
> double at Southwell *Daily Telegraph* 15 January 1994

Ideally I would like to run all 10.

> MARTIN PIPE, who had entered 10 of the 46 Cheltenham Gold Cup entries
> announced on 13 January 1994. Methinks he has designs on Michael
> Dickinson's first five record.

Look after him – he's my pet.

> JENNY PITMAN to Richard Dunwoody, who was partnering Toby Tobias in his first race for nearly two years at Wincanton on 13 January 1994. Toby finished a respectable third.

If I could have one wish granted it would be the development of an effective vaccine against equine herpes.

> JOHN DUNLOP *Sporting Life* 14 January 1994

I prefer racehorses to footballers – they don't talk back.

> Trainer and former Southampton and England footballer MICK CHANNON, dismissing rumours that he might fancy becoming Saints' manager, BBC Radio, 5 January 1994

The only way

The only way to stop jockeys abusing the rules is to disqualify the horse.

> Trainer MARY REVELEY (*Weekender* 22 January 1994), adding, 'I would rather one of mine lost a race than be subjected to excessive use of the whip.'

I just relied on basic horsemanship and did things the way I thought was right.

> SATISH SEEMAR, after his Dayflower had won at York in May 1993 to become the first British winner to be trained in Dubai

I thought we were beaten. But then I remembered who trained the horse and, believe me, that took us both to the post.

> Jockey ROY HIGGINS after riding Red Handed to a narrow victory in the 1967 Melbourne Cup, the third successive Cup win for legendary handler Bart Cummings

I'm not one for making New Year's resolutions, and although the missus would no doubt like to make one or two on my behalf she knows bloody well I won't keep them.

> DAVID NICHOLSON *Racing Post* 1 January 1993

I'm suffering from E.B. virus.

> PAUL KELLEWAY at Lingfield, explaining that it stands for Empty Boxes *Racing Post* 10 January 1994

She had bones sticking out in all directions but they told me the Duchess of Norfolk wanted her, and I liked the look in her eye – the mare's I mean.

> Veteran trainer KEN OLIVER recalling how he bought subsequent Scottish National winner Salvina for a mere £250 *Daily Telegraph* 12 January 1994

Entertrainer.

> Accurate description of trainer/impersonator Richard Phillips, coined by MARCUS ARMYTAGE *Racing Post* 29 January 1994

I could get into a fight every day with people who say 'He was a brilliant jockey but he couldn't train.'

> NELSON GUEST, former work rider for Sir Gordon Richards *Sporting Life* 31 January 1994

There are only two certainties in life – one is dying and the other is owning a winner if it is trained by Charlie Mann.

> The message inside trainer CHARLIE MANN's 1993 Christmas cards

That horse was doped and anyone who says otherwise is talking either through their hat or their backside or both.

> DAVID BARONS, trainer of 1988 Cheltenham Gold Cup flop Playschool, quoted by Jamie Reid *Independent on Sunday* 12 December 1993

American jockeys are better. They ride closer to the horse, they are neater and I think they're stronger, too.

> English trainer in America, DEREK MEREDITH *Sporting Life* November 1993

I don't know why I mentioned it – it must have been a premonition.

> JOSH GIFFORD on why he tipped 25/1 Lingfield winner General Brandy to a shooting friend *Sporting Life* 21 January 1994

I do feel sorry for the ones that can't run; they don't have the ability, but they can't help it. It's not easy being a racehorse.

> Sympathetic viewpoint (possibly not shared by those who back the ones he's talking about) expressed by New York trainer PETER FERRIOLA *New York Racing Association Media Guide* 1993

It is always important to remember that they are all different people. They've all got different habits. That's what I love about horses – their different character. Some you love and some you can't stand.

> JOHN GOSDEN, who could just as easily have been making the same remarks about owners *Pacemaker & Thoroughbred Breeder* April 1994

Captain [Ryan] Price is an incisive man of action. He met his wife Dorothy on a Sunday and married her the same week!

> BROUGH SCOTT *William Hill Racing Yearbook* 1973

We've tried everything to get them fit, short of galloping round the kitchen table.

> JACK BERRY bemoaning the wet weather at Cockerham *Sporting Life* 15 April 1994

Horses are much happier in less open spaces.

> VINCENT O'BRIEN *Racing Post* 14 April 1994

A big run from Merry Master would be a fitting finale to a 34-year career which, if nothing else, dissuaded me from ever contemplating life as a trainer.

> Jockey-writer MARCUS ARMYTAGE on his father Roddy's final runner in the Scottish National *Daily Telegraph* 16 April 1994

I'm too old to retire.

> 74-year-old US handler JIMMY CROLL *Racing Post* 20 April 1994

I understand that you have twice trained the winner of a selling steeplechase at Newton Abbot. This happens to be my fourth Gold Cup.

> JACK JARVIS to a trainer who had been casting doubt on the paddock appearance of Ocean Swell, prior to his triumph in the 1945 Ascot Gold Cup

I had three strongly fancied runners and was looking forward to celebrating my birthday in style. Two of them started favourite and all three were beaten.

> MICHAEL KAUNTZE on his failure to send out a winner on his 50th birthday in 1991 – something he has failed to do before or since *Racing Post* 20 April 1994

The council told me they didn't want the leisure centre overrun by racing. I told them that without racing it wouldn't be Lambourn.

> PETER WALWYN, who has created a racing hall of fame at the leisure centre in Lambourn where he is Chairman of the Lambourn Trainers' Association *Daily Telegraph* 23 April 1994

I've still got packets of samples at home from Henry Cecil, Michael Stoute, Geoff Wragg, Clive Brittain and a dozen other stables.

> MARTIN PIPE on how in his early days as a trainer he would visit top handlers and 'borrow' a little of the feed they were giving their charges *The Champion Trainer's Story* – Martin Pipe with Richard Pitman, Headline, 1992

I don't think one's place of work should be a total public place. I don't see any reason at all why anyone should have complete access.

> JOHN DUNLOP on the public scrutiny of trainers *Racing Post* 28 April 1994

Let us hear no more comments by trainers before the race: 'He'll be much better for the outing.' That is either an insult to the Jockey Club and to the public or the mark of a bad trainer.

> TIM FITZGEORGE-PARKER *Raceform Update* 30 April 1994

As Noel Murless used to say, when you think you've got several Derby horses, you haven't got one.

JOHN GOSDEN *Sporting Life* 29 April 1994

Born, not made

Good trainers, like good wives, are born not made. Without natural flair it is far better to keep away from racing stables and run a garage.

Chauvinistic comment by A.T. PERSSE, who died in 1960 aged 91, attributed to him by Roger Mortimer in 1979

I can remember eating some of the 50lb Cheshire cheese which is given to the owners of the first three horses in the Cup. It captured my imagination and I have always wanted to win this race. It's a fairy story I know, but sometimes they come true.

How a 24-year-old piece of cheese inspired ROBERT WILLIAMS to plot the Chester Cup victory of Doyce in 1994 (*The Times* 5 May 1994). And if the plot had failed? Simple – hard cheese!

Your horses are galloping like a lot of old gentlemen. Make them *work*.

Sound advice from SIR NOEL MURLESS to son-in-law Henry Cecil whose first 30 runners had come back losers, Rodney Masters *Racing Post* 11 May 1994

Invitations to my funeral are not going out for a while yet, anyway.

83-year-old Grand National-winning trainer NEVILLE CRUMP, 'killed off' by a Yorkshire Ridings magazine article *Weekender* 23 April 1994

I reckon I am an ordinary sort of a chap and I must certainly be approachable because punters are always approaching me after a horse of ours runs badly!

JACK BERRY *Weekender* 23 April 1994

Proper planning prevents piss-pot performance.

The motto of MICK CHANNON, revealed by fellow trainer Chris Wall *Sporting Life* 13 May 1994

I know it sounds very grand but I think we might be the horseman's horseman.

Newmarket handler CHRIS WALL using the Royal 'we' to describe his stable's training philosophy *Sporting Life* 13 May 1994

He is a great trainer, a marvellous stableman with a genuine devotion to his horses. He often seems brash and conceited and even now that he has reached his sixties he has not yet learnt when it is expedient to keep his mouth shut. He is liable to talk far too much far too loud. A fair amount of what he says is exceptionally foolish but only individuals naive to the point of idiocy take his more outrageous statements without a pinch of salt. Despite his obvious weaknesses, he has no lack of friends who swear by him and he is certainly capable of great kindness. He can, too, be very funny but most of his memorable comments would not look quite so good on paper. Appearances can be very deceptive, but his own does him absolute justice. The patrons of his stable repay study as they form a really interesting cross-section of the racing world. All in all, Ryan Price is what Edwardians used to call a 'card' and racing can never be wholly dull when he is around.

> Superb pen portrait of the controversial and outspoken Captain Ryan Price by ROGER MORTIMER in *The Flat* George Allen & Unwin, 1979

Any messing about and it was on your bike. I insisted, and still do, that all lads work hard at their stable job before they are given a chance to ride. They couldn't say, well, I can ride but I don't want to muck out. Unless they did those tasks properly they weren't given the chance to ride.

> REG HOLLINSHEAD, whose apprentices included Walter Swinburn, Kevin Darley and Willie Ryan *Sporting Life* 20 May 1994

A friend of mine calculated that in 32 years' training I've spent half my life in a car seat.

> Retiring West Country handler DAVID BARONS, who would travel far and wide for a winner *Sporting Life* 20 May 1994

He is a man of exquisite courtesy and addresses even the humbler members of the racing press as 'sir'.

> Contemporary description of JACK COLLING who trained 1953 Oaks winner Ambiguity – note the 'even', illustrating the way in which hacks were regarded even then!

You also learned how many wristwatches you could get around one horse's leg and then cover with a bandage, how many bottles of perfume you could get in the hay net without them rattling.

> ROD SIMPSON on how early days as a travelling head lad taught him about horses – and smuggling! *Mainly Fun and Horses* Marlborough, 1993

It always impresses me that someone with over 100 horses in their yard knows which is which, let alone whether they are any damn good. Nor can it help that most of them are variations on a theme of our old friend Mukkawukkashukkafukkadammah and aren't even household names in their own wadis.

> ALASTAIR DOWN in *Weekender* 28 May 1994. He may well have hit on something there, perhaps they *don't* have a clue which is which and just send out one which looks vaguely like it is ready for an outing – that at least would explain why some of the sprinters I back run like they need a two-mile trip, and vice versa!

We're both interested in one end – being winners.

> MARTIN PIPE on Richard Dunwoody *Mail on Sunday* 22 May 1994

I'd like to be remembered as a trainer who trained racehorses, not just as a footballer who won a few races.

> MICK CHANNON *Weekender* September 1993

Paul Kelleway was talking to me the other day about the fuss made of brilliant, new, young trainers. He said that if you needed to rewire your house, would you get a brilliant young electrician to do it, or someone with plenty of experience?

> IAN BALDING *Sporting Life* 25 May 1994

My horses go the same way every day; they absolutely thrive on the routine. We put a new sign up on the gallops recently and, on the first day, every horse had a good look at it and worried about it. All this talk about giving them variety is nonsense. It frightens them to death!

> JOHN DUNLOP, not a believer in variety being the spice of life, it appears *Sporting Life* 30 May 1994

Speed. More speed. Still more speed.

> The late ATTY PERSSE (1869-1960), trainer of The Tetrarch, quite possibly the fastest horse ever to grace the turf, when asked to name the three primary assets of a racehorse

OWNERS

The expectation . . . not the reality

Fiction is more fun than reality. It is a buzz when a horse runs well, but the great thing is the expectation – not the reality.

> Millionaire publisher, pornographer and owner DAVID SULLIVAN *Sporting Life* October 1993

The Marquesa de Moratalla, The Fellow's sporting owner, was at home in Paris playing bridge.

> GEOFF LESTER on the whereabouts of the owner of fourth time lucky Cheltenham Gold Cup winner The Fellow *Sporting Life* 18 March 1994

I always thought there were 200 ways you could lose a racehorse. This was 201.

> Owner VIRGINIA KRAFT PAYSON, whose Uptown Swell drowned during swimming exercise in 1990, having apparently been stung by a bee

Munro, if you don't win this race, I'll kill you.

> CLEMENT FREUD's fairly straightforward instructions to jockey Alan Munro before he went out to partner his Nagnagnag at Lingfield on 21 May 1994. Munro finished second but Freud has yet to be charged with murder *Sporting Life* 24 May 1994

I'm convinced that different trainers are best with different types of horses.

> Owner PETER SAVILL who, in September 1993, had 50 horses with 19 trainers

A mug's game

Owning racehorses is a mug's game. But I happen to love it.

> Owner PETER SAVILL

Thank you Huntingdon. Months of work from the trainer and jockey completely wasted.

> Owner of Amadeus Aes, JOHN PETERS, whose horse requires the good to firm going Huntingdon was claiming, only for jockey Nick Mann to describe part of the course as 'good to soft with heavy patches'. The horse was injured (23 October, 1993).

Next stop the Melbourne Cup.

> Perhaps the tip of the year 1993 from owner MICHAEL SMURFIT after his Vintage Crop won the Irish St Leger, and later travelled to Australia to win the Melbourne Cup

Maybe 1 per cent of the money bet on each horse should go to the owner as a performance fee.

> Californian owner E.W. 'BUD' JOHNSTON. Is the E. W. for Each Way, I wonder?

It hurts me to find I pay all the bills and I am completely ignored and the trainer is treated like a god.

> Owner TERRY WARNER on the media

Once the exclusive preserve of the rich and powerful, ownership is now a pleasure that can be enjoyed by all.

> From *The Thrill of Ownership*, the British Horseracing Board's 1993 Guide for Novice Owners. They *would* say that, wouldn't they.

When a jumper I had wouldn't take a fence, the trainer seriously told me the horse would need psychiatric treatment. I knew that was enough, and got out.

> Showbiz tycoon LORD BERNARD DELFONT explaining his exit from the game in 1988. They do say you have to be mad to become an owner – I didn't realise the horses were mad, too!

I do think that some of them – and they will remain nameless – expect too smart a lifestyle.

> Owner LORD HOWARD DE WALDEN, who has also referred to handlers as 'paid grooms' and is himself one of England's wealthiest men *Daily Express* October 1993

He was getting so fed up, this was definitely the last chance.

> CELIA MILLER, wife of owner James, who had vowed to change his racing colours if his Joy Of Freedom did not win at Folkestone on 24 May 1994 to break a barren run of almost seven years without a win since Debach Delight obliged in September 1987. It worked – the horse was a 20/1 winner (*The Independent* 25 May 1994). Mind you, given that the racing colours in question are emerald green, yellow disc and sleeves with a red cap, one might suggest that it would have been a relief to everyone else, if not the owner, had the horse been beaten!

We sometimes forget just how awesome an amount of money lies in the possession of the big-hitters in our game. To the likes of Sheikh Mohammed, Hamdan, Mana and Maktoum Al Maktoum, Khaled Abdullah and Fahd Salman, £40,000 genuinely has no more significance than the amount you or I might spend buying the kids a packet of fruit pastilles to chomp in the car.

ALASTAIR DOWN, *Weekender* 28 May 1994

We sometimes forget just how awesome an amount of money lies in the possession of the big-hitters in our game … the likes of Sheikh Mohammed

Am I buying it for resale? To breed with at stud later on? Or for an ego trip?

> Owner-trainer IVAN ALLAN's check-list of three questions he believes all owners should ask themselves before committing themselves to a purchase *Sporting Life* 25 May 1994

When we looked at buying this horse the report came back saying everything was wrong with him. So I said to my people, 'Buy him!'

> SHEIKH MOHAMMED, proving that he does have a sense of humour, after his Seismograph, trained in Dubai by Hilal Ibrahim, won Newmarket's Madagans Company Services Maiden Stakes on 28 April 1994 *The Times*

Jarvis, I fear we have got into a vein of also-rans. R.

> The entire content of a letter from former Prime Minister LORD ROSEBERY, a somewhat impatient owner, to his trainer Jack Jarvis in the early 1920s after a horse of theirs was unplaced at Lincoln – on the opening day of the season. Quoted in *The Flat* Roger Mortimer, George Allen & Unwin, 1979

I adore the horse and had my reservations about tackling such fences, but when I saw Forgive 'N' Forget break a leg in a freak accident at Cheltenham I knew that these things can happen anywhere. So I decided to give it a go.

> Realistic owner JULIET REED, owner of 1988 Grand National winner Rhyme 'N' Reason *Sporting Life*

I cry and get so worked up. In fact, talk about Becher's Brook – I'm a babbling brook.

> JULIET REED after her Rhyme 'N' Reason won the National

I don't go in for slow horses but these days they are the only races the Arabs will let us win.

> ROBERT SANGSTER after his Nomadic Way won the Cesarewitch in October 1988, Ruff's Guide *Sporting Life* 1989

I'm glad I won, because if I hadn't I'd have taken my horses away from you.

> Owner LORD JOICEY to trainer Neville Crump after his Springbok won the 1962 Hennessy Gold Cup. There's gratitude for you!

Sagacity and intelligence

We have before had occasion to compliment the sagacity and intelligence displayed by Mr Cartwright's horses. They never win when they are favourites, but always when long odds are to be obtained about them. The public ought to be grateful to them.

> Sarcastic comment by a writer in the *Sporting Life* of August 1865. How many 'Mr Cartwrights' can you spot in the game today?

It was a very good training feat by trainer Ronnie O'Leary to park the knacker's van outside the horse's box.

> Owner STEVE HAMMOND whose Concert Paper won, at Wetherby on 13 January 1994, after a three-year blank

A dead fag-end.

> Dismissive comment by Jockey Club Director of Public Affairs DAVID PIPE following a *Sunday Express* 8 September 1991 story alleging that racehorse owners were to strike

We could put our money into a building, but how long can you look at it and enjoy it? With a beautiful horse you can look and admire him or her for a long time and never be tired of it.

> SHEIKH MOHAMMED, asked 'Why racing?' by Tony Stafford, who recalled the answer in the *Daily Telegraph* 22 July 1991

I think I could have won on him.

> Over-optimistic assessment of the ease with which his Rodrigo De Triano had just won the Laurent Perrier Champagne Stakes at Doncaster, by ROBERT SANGSTER, 13 September 1991

I told him not to be such a bloody fool. I made it clear that Slip Anchor was going for the Derby, and it was highly likely he would win it. In the end I didn't have to press too hard to get my way. I think Henry knew he was talking drivel.

> Owner LORD HOWARD DE WALDEN's version of how he 'persuaded' Henry Cecil that Slip Anchor should not sidestep the Derby in favour of the St Leger, Rodney Masters, *Racing Post* 11 May 1994

I wound up in hospital with four broken ribs, but all the owner wanted to know was where his colours were and when he would get them back. He got them back all right, but they were a bit more tattered and torn than he could have bargained for.

> Jockey RICHARD FOX on one of his more sympathetic employers *Sporting Life* 7 May 1994

The Sheikh himself is 95 per cent responsible for the day-to-day training.

> News of a new string to the bow of owner SHEIKH MOHAMMED in Dubai, reported by ROBERT SANGSTER *Daily Mail* 27 November 1993

Racing is a team game and I've surrounded myself with the best players! My team is like Liverpool in the 1980s. We've got a man in every position.

> ROBERT SANGSTER *The Guardian* 1 June 1994

I'd like to find a man as good as him for a husband.

> PEGGY AUGUSTUS, owner of Husband, winner of Canada's Rothmans International at Woodbine in October 1993, which was worth $623,000 to the winner

Being an eco-friendly chap, he naturally invited Jane to share his bath bubbles. She graciously accepted. At which point enter Roger, the unsuspecting butler. With all the aplomb that Sir John Gielgud would have brought to the role he imperturbably carried on with his duties as if his lordship were alone in the tub with his rubber ducks.

> The incident which, according to gossip columnist ROSS BENSON, persuaded the Duke of Bedford's grandson, Lord Howland, to name his newly purchased racehorse Roger The Butler and to give said gentleman's gentleman a share of same *Daily Express* 12 May 1994

When the passengers start to fly the plane, that's the time to get off. If you employ experts you should leave it to them. In 34 years I've never taken a horse away from a trainer.

> ROBERT SANGSTER in conversation with John Karter *Sunday Times* 22 May 1994

It would be nice to think I might eventually be awarded a knighthood, but purely on what I have achieved in racing, not politically.

> ROBERT SANGSTER *Sunday Times* 22 May 1994

If one believed in reincarnation, a stallion job at Newmarket would be enjoyable.

> Former trainer turned owner TONY COLLINS, quizzed by the *Sporting Life* 1 June 1994 about an 'alternative career'

BREEDING

An inexact science

However many experts there are in the racing world, breeding remains an inexact science, and thank God for it . . . What a pity people don't take as much trouble with their own breeding as intelligent racehorse owners do. But then I suppose it is bordering on fascism to think like that.

JEFFREY BERNARD *The Spectator* 21 May 1994

The majority of yearlings are regrettably the product of matings designed for the catwalk rather than the race-track.

PATRICK BRAIN *Pacemaker & Thoroughbred Breeder* February 1994

There is no relationship between the inheritance of coat colour and the inheritance of racing ability.

JANE HENNING *Highflyer International Journal*, Vol. 2, Issue 8, 1994

I love the breeding and farming of horses; probably a little bit more than I like golf. Or at least as equal.

Golfer GARY PLAYER, hedging his bets *The Times* 31 May 1994

I never sell my old mares. Instead, I have them put down because I believe that, if animals do you well, you should see them out properly.

Irish breeder PAT O'KELLY *Sporting Life* October 1993

The thoroughbred exists because its selection has depended not on experts, technicians or zoologists, but on a piece of wood – the winning post of the Epsom Derby. If you base your criteria on anything else you will get something else, not the thoroughbred.

Legendary Italian breeder FEDERICO TESIO (quoted by Julian Muscat)

FOR, BY AND ABOUT JOCKEYS

I'm all right, Jack

It's certainly not gentlemanly out there. It's f*** you, I'm all right, Jack.

> GRAHAM McCOURT on the Cheltenham Festival *Sunday Times* 6 March 1994

I reckon I need 350 rides a year to break even.

> DALE GIBSON *Daily Telegraph* 4 June 1994

Because I like the food.

> TONY CULHANE explaining to Michael Parkinson why he rides in India during the winter *Daily Telegraph* 4 June 1994

That's for Mum and Dad.

> Triumphant shout from FRANKIE DETTORI after Balanchine romped home in the Oaks to give him his first Classic victory *Sporting Life* 6 June 1994

I'm a very ambitious person, but my ambitions never exceed what I feel it is possible to achieve.

> DECLAN MURPHY *Racing Post* 13 January 1994

At least when I come home from work now I won't frighten my two daughters. I just hope they don't want to be jockeys. I'm a bit chauvinistic when it comes to female jockeys. I don't like to think of them knocking their teeth out.

> 37-year-old ALLEN WEBB upon his retirement from the saddle in October 1993 to take up a job as a jockey's valet *Sporting Life*

Bloody hell. You can ride again.

> Ironic comment from JAMIE OSBORNE to Richard Dunwoody, after the latter rebounded from a quiet spell with a Southwell treble *The Independent* 22 January 1994

The connection between all those who have got to 1000, considering what it takes, is that we must all be nuts.

> STAN MELLOR, the first jump jockey to reach 1000 winners, after Richard Dunwoody joined him, Scudamore and Francome *The Independent* 31 January 1994

I just think it's a load of bollocks.

> RICHARD DUNWOODY on criticism of his riding abilities *The Independent* 22 January 1994

When it comes to his cash he's astute – or should I say tight as they come.

> Trainer PETER MONTEITH on up and coming jockey Tony Dobbin – a budding Lester?

I'm a boring bastard, me.

> Jockey TONY DOBBIN *Racing Post* 5 February 1994

My ability to finesse the turf, my patience and ability to communicate with the horse enables me to get there first.

> French-born jockey JEAN-LUC SAMYN who has scored a string of successes in New York, when asked about his strongest assets as a jockey. He obviously overlooked his modesty *NYRA Media Guide* 1993

470 winners and 5000 losers.

> Self-effacing career description by former jockey turned media pundit RICHARD PITMAN

Do something about them or I will do it myself.

> Distraught at being berated by disgruntled punters after he had ridden a series of beaten favourites, Aussie jockey JIM CASSIDY issued an ultimatum to stewards at Warwick Farm, Sydney in February 1992

I wish you got that sort of money for finishing last every day.

> KEVIN MANNING who rode 300/1 outsider of six, Barry's Run, to his expected sixth place in the Irish Derby but collected IR£9000 for the owner in so doing, 30 June 1991

I won't starve because I have three lurchers and they will keep me in rabbits.

> Recently retired CHRIS GRANT *Racing Post* 23 April 1994

Nowadays jockeys – in addition to absurd retainers – are given perfectly farcical presents for winning quite unimportant races, which in practice only spoils them, and does much harm.

> 'AUDAX' in *Horse and Hound* – from 1922. Some things don't change!

Aaaah . . .

> Gold Cup-winning jockey ADAM KONDRAT, Polish born, shrugging off his arch-critic John McCririck's grovelling apologies for ever doubting his abilities, in the winners' enclosure *The Times* 18 March 1994

I could feel something tugging at my leg and when I looked down he had the number cloth and the back of my boot in his mouth. I kicked out at him and luckily he let go. I'm fatter than usual at the moment and there is plenty of me to get hold of. Anyway, I won.

> MICHAEL ROBERTS, who found rival Arcadian Heights hungry for success at all costs at Doncaster. Unsympathetic Walter Swinburn, riding Arcadian Heights, commented: 'He just fancied a bit of African bacon' *Daily Mirror* 20 March 1992

I saved up £25 from milking cows but that wasn't enough to buy the pony. That's where my mum's fridge-freezer came in. I took a chance and nicked it to clinch the deal. I'm always asked if I repaid my mum. I'm afraid I didn't, but I did get her a new washing machine instead!

> Classic-winning jockey JASON WEAVER on how a mountain pony called Volvo tempted him into a criminal act before his frozen assets helped him clean up as a rider *The Sun* 29 April 1994

I did it to give the crowd a laugh.

> 61-year-old jockey DENNIS TURNER who returned to the saddle after a twenty-year lay-off on the spur of the moment, just to make sure a race at the Devon & Somerset point-to-point was not a walkover. In fact, it was – when Dennis and Shaugh Moor finished miles behind *Racing Post* 10 May 1994

I'll not lose too much sleep.

> PAT EDDERY on his split with owner Prince Khalid Abdullah *Sporting Life* 13 May 1994

The worst days

The worst days are when you drive a hundred miles or more and find a meeting has been abandoned. Nobody pays you for that.

> SIMON McNEILL on life as one of the unsung heroes of the racing game *The Times* 28 December 1993

Life in the shadow of a famous father is tough. Even when I won the Arc an old lady came up to me and said 'you will never be as good as your father'.

> ERIC SAINT-MARTIN, who won the 1993 Arc on Urban Sea

Everyone thought I was a four stone better jockey two minutes after the race than I was two minutes before it.

> GRAHAM BRADLEY on the reaction to his brilliant 1993 Martell Hurdle win on Morley Street *Racing Post* 17 February 1994

I'd hate to find myself in trouble if I were to ride in the race.

> Recently retired jockey HYWEL DAVIES, unable to ride in the race at Chepstow named after him, having set up a tipping service *Sporting Life* 27 February 1994

It was a performance more associated with a butcher boy than a future champion. Forget the waving, he beat his horse up!

GEOFF LESTER of the *Sporting Life* (17 January 1994) on Adrian Maguire's controversial ride on Ramstar at Warwick in which he wielded his whip on over 20 occasions

You're far too young to retire. You'll probably get killed in the car on the way home!

Jockey NEALE DOUGHTY to 32-year-old Andy Orkney who had just announced his retirement from the saddle, December 1993

I couldn't survive. When I broke it all down, I was earning just £20 for a day's work. And that would be two or three days a week, if I was lucky. I'd get to the end of the month and my Weatherby's cheque would arrive and I wouldn't have the money to pay off my Access bill for the petrol.

Jockey ALLEN WEBB, explaining why he quit the saddle (*Sporting Life* October 1993). It isn't all glamour and glitz.

I've been off it for a year. Drink was killing me, my liver was in a terrible state. It was a bad old do and in many ways it's a miracle I'm still here.

Former champion jump jockey TERRY BIDDLECOMBE *The Times* 7 March 1994

We immediately crossed one another off our Christmas lists.

PETER SCUDAMORE referring to his relationship with Jenny Pitman following the Cheltenham Gold Cup incident in which her Golden Freeze 'spoiled' hot favourite Carvills Hill's chance by jumping alongside him *Daily Mail* October 1993

I've given Dean an old penny I found on the floor of the weighing-room.

Generous reward by GRAHAM BRADLEY whose presumed-missing contacts book turned up in the car of colleague Dean Gallagher in October 1993

I felt myself hoping that Fontwell was off. I had always loved going there. If I wanted Fontwell to be off, I had no chance of getting round Plumpton!

A brutally honest RICHARD ROWE announcing his February 1991 decision to quit the saddle

Then where the hell have I been for a week?

> Yorkshire jockey JIM SNOWDEN, who was partial to the odd tipple, upon arriving at Chester in the 1880s to take part in a big meeting – only to be informed that it had taken place seven days earlier

I was here an hour and a half before racing and I had a doze. When I woke up I was a minute late to weigh out.

> Sleepy GRAHAM BRADLEY whose pre-racing snooze meant he missed his one booked ride at Worcester on Macedonas who, of course, duly won! Clearly not a man to entrust with your nap! *Sporting Life* 19 May 1994

Thinking of myself

No – I was thinking of myself.

> Jockey ERIC SAINT-MARTIN who had just ridden Urban Sea to win the 1993 Arc, when asked: 'Were you thinking of your father?'

He has to have a challenge, and golf has provided it.

> STEVE CAUTHEN's wife Amy on the ex-champ's new interest *Daily Mirror* 13 December 1993

I didn't want to get to the stage where my boots were hung up and I was still in them.

> Retiring jockey S.J. O'NEILL 1993

The end of the road is just around the corner, but which one I don't know.

> Jockey WILLIAM FISHER HUNTER CARSON OBE, 1993

I never used an agent while riding because I was too mean to pay out 10 per cent of my earnings to them. I felt I could do a better job myself.

> PETER SCUDAMORE *Daily Mail* 9 December 1993

I'll be glad to reach 50 and call it a day.

> 41-year-old PAT EDDERY *Sunday Express* October 1993

Retire? In seven years' time when I'm 45.

> MICHAEL ROBERTS *Pacemaker & Thoroughbred Breeder* October 1993

I will.

> JACKIE OLIVER to boyfriend Simon Edwards' proposal of marriage – after he had ridden his first winner at Kilworthy point-to-point in March 1993 – without which she had refused to get wed

I could retire.

> STEVE CAUTHEN in January after negotiations for his 1993 contract with Sheikh Mohammed collapsed. I wonder if he will?

I deeply regret the incident.

> RICHARD DUNWOODY after being arrested for disorderly behaviour following the Jockeys Association Awards ceremony in London in March 1993

I have always entertained the idea of riding over hurdles and I have schooled for David Nicholson.

> Top flat jock WALTER SWINBURN *Sporting Life* October 1993

I have to ride out every morning and do odd jobs in the afternoon to keep afloat.

> Former glamour girl GEE ARMYTAGE, finding the going tough *The Sun* 25 November 1993

You could say I'm in the middle lane of the motorway with my indicator on to go right.

> Up and coming Irish jump jockey MICK FITZGERALD, 9 December 1993

I'm riding out for every stable bar Bethlehem at the moment

> Does this mean DEAN McKEOWN is cribbing rides? *Sporting Life* 27 June 1994

I'm a dinosaur in the weighing room. With all these agents and mobile phones about, it's like a telephone exchange in there.

> 37-year-old jockey ALLEN WEBB, retiring in October 1993 *Sporting Life*

My whole career seems to have been a case of always threatening to, but never quite making it.

> HYWEL DAVIES, announcing his retirement *Racing Post* 19 January 1994

I spoke to Martin's father David, who told me he thinks that all jockeys are idiots and that I should have retired a year earlier than I did.

> PETER SCUDAMORE revealing that his offer to return to the saddle for the 1994 Cheltenham Festival to ride the Pipe stable runners, after their jockey Richard Dunwoody had been suspended, was 'politely' turned down *Daily Mail* 5 March 1994

For their three-month break the luminous little big men of the saddle prefer to put their feet up, or play the squire, or count their money, or refurbish their saunas or, in most cases, earn themselves a suntan as they gallop off into warmer tropical sunsets filling their already bulging saddlebags with yet more bundles of booty from rides around warmer paddocks than Britain's.

> FRANK KEATING on why stretching the flat season to fill the calendar year hasn't pleased everyone *The Guardian* 24 March 1994

Long-serving footballers and cricketers have testimonials to give them a nice cushion when they quit the sport. I don't see why testimonials shouldn't become a natural 'pay-off' for jockeys too, as a way of giving them a leg-up into the next phase of their working life.

> Jockey RICHARD FOX 19 March 1994

The horse is Sam's Heritage and it's going to win.

> Jockey JULIAN PRITCHARD, explaining to the traffic cop who'd pulled him over why he was in a hurry to get to Exeter races. It did, at 10/1 *Racing Post* 26 March 1994

I told Nicky that if we won we'd get engaged – we'd talked about it but had no money.

> Jockey JASON WEAVER, describing negotiations with his girlfriend before he won the 1993 Wokingham at Royal Ascot on Nagida *Sporting Life* 24 March 1994

If you took all of the money, the fortunes if you will, that I earned last year and gave them to me and, at the same time, took away the riding and winning of races, I'd look for another job.

> Top US rider PAT DAY whose career earnings stood at $125,821,036 when he made this comment in 1993

It is money which speaks a lot there, whereas in jump racing we know it is a more dangerous profession and we help each other. We are a lot more conscious of that.

> Polish-born rider of The Fellow, ADAM KONDRAT, on flat racing

I feel like I'm a businessman riding horses and not someone who would ride just anything... . Prize money is more important to me than numbers of winners.

> DECLAN MURPHY to Andy Orkney *Sporting Life* 27 May 1994

I didn't exactly become resentful in the early days but there were times when I wondered how long it would take. It was always just a case of pushing myself and saying hello again and again, until people recognised me. They even used to turn the other way when they saw me coming.

> MICHAEL ROBERTS on the days in the late 1970s before he was accepted in Britain *Benson & Hedges Racing Year* Pelham Books, 1989

When other jockeys are beaten on hot favourites you see punters swear at them. When it happens to me they seem to accept it. They understand I am doing my best.

> WILLIE CARSON, a man who has clearly never stood in a betting shop and listened to the reasoned, understanding, sympathetic remarks from those punters who have invested a bob or two on him when he's riding a well-fancied but beaten horse *Sunday Express* 24 April 1993

I think my saving grace as a jockey was determination, backed up by bravery bordering on stupidity . . . I fell off more times than I stayed on, yet doggedly refused to let go of the reins . . . As for race riding, I admit I lacked the basic skills, although I got quite good at falling.

> Now you know why he made it to the top as a trainer rather than a jockey. MARTIN PIPE, whose riding career total of wins stands at . . . one. *The Champion Trainer's Story*, Martin Pipe with Richard Pitman, Headline, 1992

I have been taking water pills for the last 18 months to keep my weight down. In the last two months of the season I probably took 150 pills to keep riding. But my body is not losing weight like it used to. If I keep taking pills I could be dead by the time I'm 30. I'm definitely going to miss riding but my health must come first. Doctors have told me I shouldn't be doing what I am doing and to find another career path.

> New Zealand jockey MATTHEW ENRIGHT, in his mid-twenties, with 340 winners to his credit, announcing his decision to quit the game before it quit him *New Zealand News* 13 October 1993

It's a great thrill to partner my first winner but I've decided not to renew my jockey's licence because of my weight.

> Possibly the first jockey ever to celebrate his first-ever winner and then announce his retirement, 21-year-old Irishman CONOR QUINLAN after winning on Muskora at Exeter on 27 April 1994 *Racing Post*

If I start hearing people saying I've gone and I don't feel right myself, I'll pack up.

> PAT EDDERY's philosophy which, if copied by us mere mortals, would have seen us pack it in years ago! *The Independent* 28 April 1994

I would like to see the jockeys' title decided on prize money won during the period from 1 January to 31 December. This would level itself out during the year and be fairer to everybody.

> WALTER SWINBURN *Weekender* 30 April 1994

Apparently I am a cowardly little shit.

> Widely tipped to be a future champion jump jockey, 13-year-old PAUL HORRIGAN after a training session at Enda Bolger's. *Sporting Life* 25 April 1994

He will definitely be champion [jump] jockey.

> ADRIAN MAGUIRE on 13-year-old Irish youngster Paul Horrigan, son of trainer Michael *The Times* 6 January 1994

Get a good agent. Times have changed since I started. Agents were unheard of then, but if you haven't got a good agent today, you are not going to make it.

> The retiring 'hard-man' of the jockey world, CHRIS GRANT, with advice to newcomers *Sporting Life* 29 April 1994

It's certainly much more demanding than being a boxer, a racing driver, an athlete or whatever. In these sports they tune up for a specific event – but jockeys are on the go seven days a week and it is very physically punishing.

> Ex-jock JIMMY LINDLEY on the physical prowess of his modern-day counterparts *Racing Post* 13 May 1994

There is not much to being a jockey. You're not really an athlete, the horse does all the work.

> Olympic gold medallist DAVID HEMERY in conversation with Peter Scudamore who recorded the remark in the *Daily Mail* 9 July 1994

The best

He was certainly the best jockey I've ever seen in my lifetime.

> LESTER PIGGOTT attending Charlie Smirke's funeral *Sporting Life* 1 January 1994

I told the Sheikh that I was the only man to ride him a Derby winner in England.

> RICHARD FOX, adding that it was Orpheus in the Northumberland Plate, the Pitmen's Derby, thus confusing Sheikh Mohammed *Sporting Life* 1 January 1994

Like a good brand of food, Dunwoody is a good commodity, so he will be easy to sell.

> Richard Dunwoody's newly appointed agent ROBERT PARSONS *The Independent* 5 January 1994

No one knew who I was in the pre-race parade. But when I arrived back in the mounting yard I was suddenly mobbed by 150 relations I never knew I had.

> Jockey JOHN LETTS recalling his 1972 Melbourne Cup victory on Piping Lane *Daily Telegraph* November 1993

When I came to England first I was 14. Living in digs in Newmarket, and I couldn't speak a word of English. I didn't learn English, I just picked it up as I went along. I think the first word I ever learned was goodbye.

> Italian-born jockey FRANKIE DETTORI *Daily Telegraph* November 1993

I can assure you that Richard Dunwoody will be with us next season despite all the nonsense that has been written. The only way he will not be with us is if he leaves of his own accord.

> DAVID PIPE, father of Martin, at Exeter *Racing Post* 3 January 1994

The funniest thing is seeing Richard and Adrian together when they've had a couple of drinks. Adrian will tell Richard that he's the best and Richard will reply: 'No, Adrian, you're the best.' They can go on like that for hours.

> She should know. CAROL DUNWOODY, wife of Richard, *Sunday Telegraph* 29 May 1994

And that's Frankie Dettori's 52nd winner of the season.

> Racecourse commentator at Doncaster making a unique announcement for the first day of any turf flat season as Frankie partnered Pay Homage to victory, having already chalked up 51 all-weather winners, 24 March 1994

The St Mark's Square Bum Pincher.

Colourful nickname for Frankie Dettori *The Punter* fanzine, January 1994

He could ride his own horse and the horse next to him, too.

Tribute to Angel Cordero, Jr from Cuban-born New York trainer LUIS SOSA BARRERA *NYRA Media Guide* 1993

Maguire also has great technical ability, loving hands on the withers and that indefinable quality of all riding greats. The ability to communicate his insatiable ambition to the most reluctant mounts. Maybe, like Dr Doolittle, he simply talks to the animals.

ROY COLLINS on Adrian Maguire, *Today* October 1993

He didn't want to be a jockey very much after he broke his back, yet was champion four times. He was very, very dubious about becoming a trainer – and look at him, two Grand Nationals in his first two years.

> STAN MELLOR on Fred Winter *William Hill Racing Yearbook* 1973

Some people like him, some don't, but all the horses think he's great.

> JIMMY LINDLEY on Willie Carson *Sporting Life* 25 May 1994

If they keep oiling him he'll go on for ever.

> PAT EDDERY on Willie Carson *Racing Post* 25 May 1994

When I am asked who I feared most ranging upsides me in a race, most expect me to answer Dunwoody or Francome, but to match the mounts of Gary Moore, stride for stride, down the hill at Plumpton, trying to ask your mount to stand off as far away from the fence as Gary's, I had to equal one of the bravest riders on the circuit.

> PETER SCUDAMORE on jockey turned trainer Gary Moore *Daily Mail* 28 May 1994

I will not be going to these extremes again. If I tried to keep this pace up I'd only be able to ride for another two seasons.

> RICHARD DUNWOODY after clinching the William Hill-sponsored Jockey Championship for season 1993-94 *The Sun* 6 June 1994

I shall be trying twice as hard next season.

> ADRIAN MAGUIRE, suggesting that Mr Dunwoody may *have* to go to those extremes! *The Sun* 6 June 1994

I feel Adrian is the moral winner.

> Surely not the sour grapes comment that it seemed, by Maguire's agent DAVE ROBERTS, whose £8000 phone bill failed to land the title for the young pretender *The Times* 6 June 1994

If you want to be a jockey

If you want to be a jockey, it's no good living in Scotland.

> Advice unlikely to endear WILLIE CARSON to the SNP! *The Scotsman* 1 June 1994

Jockeys are probably the only professional sportsmen who haven't got trainers to help them with their technique.

YOGI BREISNER, former Olympic three-day-eventer turned equine adviser to jockeys/trainers

What we are trying to do is make sure that a chap who goes round is not as high as a kite and putting everybody else at risk.

DR MICHAEL TURNER, chief medical adviser to the Jockey Club, on drug tests for jockeys *The Times* 18 January 1994

We are drying out jockeys in the same way we are drying out people for other organisations I am looking at.

DR MICHAEL TURNER, chief medical adviser to the Jockey Club *The Times* 18 January 1994

I've decided to change the way I use my whip. I shall just flick them with my stick in the backhand position, even though it will mean lazy horses running up to 70-80 per cent of their ability.

Horses like that will completely take the mickey when they know they won't be getting a smack. They won't be coming out of third gear, but at least I'll be out of danger of getting into any more trouble.

Jockey CARL LLEWELLYN, after being cautioned for the third time over his whip technique in October 1993

The teachers are very co-operative, and they all know how keen I am on racing and on trying to become a jockey.

16-year-old schoolboy MATTHEW KNEAFSEY who missed his mock O-level science exam at Huntington Comprehensive School near York, to ride fourth-placed Sporting Spirit at Southwell in late 1993. On 7 January 1994 he partnered the horse to a 50/1 win and pronounced himself 'gobsmacked'.

When I was a jockey I know I rode a few that had been got at.

REG AKEHURST *Daily Express* 6 January 1994

To call me a butcher – it hurt me so much. You don't devote your whole life to horses if you don't like them. All I want is to get the best out of them, not to cause them unnecessary pain. Racehorses eat like kings and live in houses fit for queens.

ADRIAN MAGUIRE, after being accused of over-zealous use of the whip *The Independent* 12 February 1994

I think veterinary science, not surgery, is 200 years behind the times.

> Trainer JOHN UPSON after a top veterinary college informed him there was nothing wrong with Very Very Ordinary, who pulled up bleeding and coughing *Sporting Life* 22 February 1994

I sent him to Bristol University to be checked over and they said he would never win a race.

> Trainer BILL PREECE after his Jon's Choice added a 3/1 Wolverhampton victory to an earlier 33/1 win at the same track *Sporting Life* 21 February 1994

The only logical way to measure a rider's effectiveness is to examine how horses have performed for him compared with their performance for other jockeys.

> JOHN WHITLEY *Computer Racing Form* February 1994

I read that Carl Llewellyn had been trying to get back to ride in the National with a broken bone in his leg. Nice try, Carl, but I always knew you never had a leg to stand on.

> RICHARD FOX *Sporting Life* 16 April 1994

The trouble with so many young jockeys is that they're scared to talk to the best jockeys.

> DAVID BRIDGWATER, who had no such inhibitions *Racing Post* 20 April 1994

One way of ensuring they have this period of recuperation is to stipulate when a jockey receives a licence that if he obtains 300 rides in a season there must be a mandatory period of a month when he is not allowed to ride in this country.

> Well-meaning but clearly flawed suggestion from PETER SCUDAMORE to combat the introduction of all-year-round racing and eventual exhaustion for jockeys – who would just fly off to ride abroad, anyway *Daily Mail* 23 April 1994

More and more racing consumers are of the opinion, rightly or wrongly, that when jockeys go to sleep with the proverbial ton in hand on the rails, in a small field of three to eight runners, and make no effort to extricate the horse, this is often due to the effects of drugs or alcohol.

> BOSCO EGAN *Racing Post* 8 April 1994

He rates himself as a footballer and went to school in London with Paul Ince, whom he earnestly believes was inferior. Honest!

CHRIS HAWKINS on Gary 'Angry Ant' Bardwell, 4ft 8in, the great lost talent of British soccer *The Guardian* 5 May 1994

Racing is organised in such a way that an ageing jockey's decline will tend to be masked and an emerging talent's success delayed by the perpetuation of riding arrangements which give the older jockey more winning opportunities.

DAVID ASHFORTH *Sporting Life* 7 May 1994

Ride the race to suit the horse and not the horse to suit the race.

DECLAN MURPHY, quoted by fellow jock Andy Orkney *Sporting Life* 5 May 1994

Frankie!

PAUL EDDERY'S, infant son, asked by Brough Scott, 'Who's the best jockey?' on *Channel 4 Racing* (7 July 1994) after Dad had won the July Cup

While the history of Britain's oldest racecourse stretches back some way, the same cannot be said of old Pat's memory, and he has a reputation for deeming the last decent performance he has seen as the greatest ever. Racegoers are by now able to mouth along with his slogan, the one that is a dream to sofa salesmen: 'That's the best one I've ever sat on'.

The Independent's RICHARD EDMONDSON casting aspersions on the reliability of a certain Mr Eddery's recall, 10 May 1994

They are both great jockeys and good friends of mine. But there is a difference. If you are down at the start and ask Adrian what his plans are, he will tell you. Ask Richard and he will mutter something unintelligible. He can't bear to give an inch to anybody.

JAMIE OSBORNE on the Maguire–Dunwoody rivalry *Sunday Times* 15 April 1994

Paul lived with me and went to school from here. But he only attended in the afternoon. I arranged it with the headmaster who was a keen racing man.

> REG HOLLINSHEAD on the unorthodox schooling arrangements of then 14-year-old Paul Eddery who was apprenticed to him *Sporting Life* 20 May 1994

Even in retirement you can get 'jocked off'. John Francome rang me to ask if he could take my mount on Talented Ting to enable him to carry a camera on his helmet for *Channel 4 Racing*.

> PETER SCUDAMORE on how he came to lose his ride in a charity race at Lingfield on 21 May 1994

People try to put human emotions into horses but it's a mistake. Horses like to wake up at 7 o'clock in the morning, know they're going to be fed at 7.30, have a swim at the same time every day and then be fed in the evening. They like to be bored and feel confident in their surroundings.

> PETER SCUDAMORE to Sue Lawley on *Desert Island Discs* 29 May 1994

Once, Richard received a trophy for Michael at Longchamp while his brother was taking a shower. Even their father Barry was deceived as he stood on the victory rostrum.

> JONATHAN POWELL on the benefits of having an identical twin brother for jockeys Michael and Richard Hills *Sunday Express* 29 May 1994

OFFICIALDOM

Jobs for the boys

Betting Intelligence Officers? It is just jobs for the boys. What a waste of money. All they are doing is giving the stewards an idea if a horse is drifting. Any of the ordinary starting price boys can do that. When the villainy was going on at Lingfield, you never saw a Betting Intelligence Officer. They are just a waste of time – 14 grand a year and a car – just a waste!

> Top southern racecourse bookmaker JOE BATES who is less than impressed with the BIOs. *BOS* magazine, May/June 1994

Once again, it looks as if there are two sets of rules – one for the big boys and one for the rest. It's diabolical.

> Trainer PETER CHAPPLE-HYAM on the decision to permit a Henry Cecil runner, whose entry had been late, to compete in the Musidora Stakes *Racing Post* 13 May 1994

I was two minutes late in declaring Kinda Groovy for a race here [Sedgefield] last month. Weatherby's wouldn't have it, but then last week they go and accept Henry Cecil's declaration for Cambrel at York after he was a few minutes late.

> Stockton-on-Tees milkman/trainer IAN PARK *Sporting Life* 19 May 1994

My own view is that they should be banned for life from ever officiating at a race meeting and that their only future connection with the turf should be as gardeners!

> ALAN SMITH on the five Curragh stewards who failed to hold an enquiry into the 1994 Irish 1000 Guineas when winner Mehthaaf, mount of Willie Carson, appeared to bump third-placed Relatively Special. There was widespread surprise that no enquiry took place and the Turf Club later criticised their stewards *Weekender* 29 May 1994

It might be thought that arrangements whereby a punter could place a bet with a bookmaker, watch the race and then have the option of cancelling the wager if his selection lost would be so ridiculous that even Monty Python would reject the script.

> TOM KELLY of BOLA (Betting Office Licensees Association) exposing a proposed piece of European Commission gobbledegook which threatened to produce a punters' paradise! *Sporting Life* 12 May 1994

That is the most ridiculous rule I have ever heard.

> Jockey WILLIE RYAN after his mount, 11/4 second favourite Loxandra, was banned from racing because she had damaged her stall at Salisbury, yet was ruled to have come under orders thus costing punters their stake money – although most major bookies took it upon themselves to refund the cash *Sporting Life* 28 May 1994

The Jockey Club have issued a writ against the Texan who introduced Cabbage Patch dolls. They claim they have been making them for years – and calling them stewards.

> Infamous 1983 comment by JOHN FRANCOME. The dolls seem to have disappeared; not so the stewards.

An abuse of power.

> MICHAEL STOUTE's opinion of the action of handicapper Richard Dangar in putting up that handler's Dahyan by 18lb after he had landed a gamble from 14/1 to 5/1, and commenting: 'That is the sort of thing that makes handicappers sit up and take notice' *The Times* 18 May 1994

I object strongly. I'm not a naughty schoolboy and expect to be trusted when doing a responsible job. The whole thing was handled extremely badly. Drinking is not allowed in the Stewards' Room and it's our guests who would suffer – the Queen Mother is a frequent guest and wouldn't get her gin and tonic.

> Former jockey turned sculptor and Windsor steward PHILLIP BLACKER on the bid by course manager Sally Dingle to ban alcohol from the stewards' hospitality area *Daily Express* 4 May 1994

If the Jockey Club's long history tells us anything, it is that most of its daftest decisions have been taken to satisfy ill-informed public concern.

> GREG WOOD *The Independent* 9 May 1994

The Jockey Club now judges distances by examining the timing band on the photo-finish print and allowing for five lengths per second. The record time for five furlongs at Epsom, achieved in 1960, is 53.6 sec, a speed of over 60ft per second. By the Jockey Club's reckoning, the horse concerned must have been 12ft long. No wonder the handicap ratings have deteriorated in recent years: the horses have shrunk!

> R. FAIRLESS of Woking in a letter to the *Racing Post* 9 May 1994. Perhaps they'll make a movie of it – Honey I Shrunk the Nags.

I remember they asked me if I could ride, as if that was anything to do with it. I asked them if Jeremy Tree could ride. Unless you are a jockey or from public school they think you know nothing about horses. Well, what jockey apart from Geoff Lewis is a good flat trainer? This attitude is an insult to our intelligence.

> MICK CHANNON on his rejection upon first applying for a trainer's licence on the grounds of lack of experience *Sunday Express* 1 May 1994

Use of the whip

Jockey Club amendments to the rules on the use of the whip caused controversy in autumn 1993:

They listened to public pressure more than the view within racing.

> MICHAEL CAULFIELD, secretary of the Jockeys' Association *Pacemaker & Thoroughbred Breeder*

It is my personal feeling that the whip does more harm than good.

> PAUL COLE

I'd be delighted not to use the whip if we got the same result, but we don't.

> Jockey CARL LLEWELLYN

I think jockeys will really struggle with the new rule but it is going to be for the better.

> REG HOLLINSHEAD

The number of times you hit them is irrelevant compared to how hard you hit them.

> GEOFF LEWIS

I don't think they should take too much notice of the RSPCA. The whip is not a big problem and racehorses are the best looked after animals in the world.

PAT EDDERY *Sunday Express* October 1993

Blatant disregard

Newcastle Clerk of the Course, David Parmley, was confident they'd be able to race. *Morning Line* reported his confidence to viewers on the programme on Saturday 27 November 1993. A couple of hours later the meeting was abandoned.

It showed a blatant disregard for punters and professionals.

PETER SCUDAMORE *Daily Mail* 2 December 1993

It was so stupid for would-be Newcastle racegoers to complain when the Clerk of the Course was doing his damnedest to provide Saturday sport but was frustrated by the weather.

TIM FITZGEORGE-PARKER *Raceform Update*

This has to go down as one of the worst cases of misinformation of all time.

DAVID SMALLEY *Raceform Update*

Newcastle has an attitude problem.

Trainer NEVILLE CALLAGHAN

This incident illustrates that some racing officials are a long way from adopting the accepted practice in other entertainment industries: that the paying customer is king.

JULIAN MUSCAT *Weekender* 4 December

Given the same conditions and evidence I would do the same again.

Unrepentant Newcastle Clerk of the Course DAVID PARMLEY

It's all very amateurish.

Shadow cabinet minister ROBIN COOK who turned up at Newcastle

As far as punters are concerned, Tattersalls Committee is little better than a kangaroo court, a Star Chamber whose proceedings would be struck down – as contrary to every principle of natural justice – by any court of law.

This is the kind of thing that would fit well in a Third World dictatorship. It rides roughshod over every principle of justice.

> Chairman of the National Association for the Protection of Punters, MARK COTON, explaining his view of the Tattersalls Committee which sits in secret and is not required to give reasons for the decisions it takes when adjudicating on betting disputes *Sporting Life* October 1993

Do race times really matter?

> CAPTAIN NICK LEES, Clerk of the Course at Newmarket, after the last race on Cesarewitch day 1993 was 22 minutes late, reported by David Smalley, October 1993. They probably do matter if you have a train to catch!

It is remarkable how exact RHT were in their bid. It certainly strikes me as a carve-up.

> Labour MP ALAN MEALE's thoughts on Racecourse Holdings Trust's purchase of United Racecourses Epsom, Sandown, Kempton Park, reported by John Karter *Sunday Times* 27 March 1994

It is noticeable that these trainers and jockeys picked out under the non-triers rules at the moment are usually the less fashionable ones.

> MARK POPHAM *Weekender* 29 January 1994

I carried out my normal pre-race checks, but was not aware that Lady Broker had won a race the previous day.

> Wolverhampton Clerk of the Course GRAHAM WILKS, after Lady Broker had been permitted to start in and 'win' a race carrying 6lb less than necessary. Bets were settled on the outcome of the race for which the winner's disqualification at a later date was inevitable. The horse had been favourite and another excuse put forward by the officials when the error was pointed out was that as the race was televised it would have been impractical to delay it, January 1994

It will help the handicappers and, perhaps, the upsurge of spread-betting on the distances is also a factor.

> Judge MALCOLM HANCOCK on the introduction of additional official winning distances. The Jockey Club paying attention to betting needs? Whatever next! *Sporting Life* 24 March 1994

Everyone hates me, and I like it.

> The 'Dictator of Epsom', HENRY MAYSON DORLING, Clerk of the Course at Epsom from 1873 to 1919. Wonder if he was related to John McCririck, or was a Millwall fan?

Enough is enough

No horses of mine will be trained here, and no horses of mine will race here. It is very sad – but I have reached the stage where I cannot expose the people who work with me or myself to this sort of situation again.

Enough is enough. I don't think I should expose myself to another case after two in eight years.

> The AGA KHAN at a press conference at the Savoy Hotel in December 1990 announcing that after the Jockey Club disqualified his 1989 Oaks winner Aliysa after the longest disciplinary committee hearing in history, he would no longer be involved in British racing

Frankly, some of the big boys have missed out and now they are moaning.

> CHARLES CYZER, pouring scorn on demands for a supplementary stage for the Derby *Racing Post* 20 May 1994

The flashing lights could not be seen in the bright daylight and the klaxons petrified the horses. So it was decided that the best system was still the flag system.

> The Jockey Club's spokesman DAVID PIPE in April 1993 describing tests of new recall systems carried out at Newbury in the early eighties. It's a wonder traffic lights ever caught on, isn't it, if lights couldn't be seen in broad daylight? *Racing Post*

Lester Piggott, Jeff King and John Francome rolled into one would not have won on the horse. I always ride to win.

> PETER SCUDAMORE in January 1988, after being fined £300 for 'not having made sufficient effort to secure the best possible placing' on Arbitrage at Newbury, Ruff's Guide *Sporting Life* 1989

What else could we do – it's not Cheltenham, so we couldn't jump them!

> MICHAEL ROBERTS after winning the Festival Stakes at Goodwood in May 1988, on Mtoto, only for the race to be voided when the runners were unable to take the true course because of incorrectly placed marker dolls *Sporting Life*

Officialdom's refusal to pee into a bottle from time to time is as myopic as Mr Magoo.

> Jockey ANDY ORKNEY in the *Sporting Life* 18 April 1994 on the Jockey Club refusal to countenance drugs testing for racecourse officials

Keeping the public better informed must be a No. 1 priority for Britain's racecourses.

> DEREK THOMPSON advocating that announcements should be made informing racegoers of the well-being or otherwise of jockeys and horses which have fallen *Sporting Life* 16 April 1994

I wish to have the same procedures for officials in case their performance is impaired . . . especially if they have a drink at lunchtime.

> MICHAEL CAULFIELD of the Jockeys Association commenting on dope testing for jockeys to Richard Edmondson of *The Independent* 17 December 1993

As a jockey I rarely agreed with any decision that went against me. I felt the stewards lacked the knowledge or understanding of the sport to understand my predicament. They were, after all, at best only amateur riders, some of whom would not even be allowed to ride out for some of the stables I rode for.

> PETER SCUDAMORE *Daily Mail* October 1993

It has been 62 years since mechanical timing first became a reality, and all but 16 British racecourses still rely on hand-timing!

> TONY HARBIDGE *Racing Post* 20 April 1994

It did take a little time to quantify what offence – careless, or irresponsible riding – Parkin had actually committed. And the stewards found that Parkin was careless rather than irresponsible. They felt that the interference had been caused by misjudgement rather than by intent. It was also felt that the winner's placing had not been improved by the incident and therefore he kept the race.

> Stipendiary steward ROBERT STOPFORD after history was made at Pontefract when the first interpretation of new interference rules enabled a jockey to be banned for careless riding but his mount allowed to retain first place *Racing Post* 20 April 1994

There are men who have grown old, with their faculties impaired through age, who, nevertheless, expect as a right to be invited to officiate. They will expect it until they die. Some of them are notorious as backers. They like to back winners, which means they must accept confidences from individuals whose horses must come under their notice. How is it possible in human nature for them to be impartial?

> Slightly critical view of stewards by SIDNEY GALTREY, for many years racing correspondent of the *Daily Telegraph*, in his 1934 book *Memoirs of a Racing Journalist*

Stewards are, on the whole, simple folk. Most of them come from a social class in which inbreeding has taken its toll.

> PAUL HAIGH *Racing Post* 23 April 1994

Eventually the pool from which stewards were selected was extended beyond the registered blind, the chronically inbred and those whose ear trumpets or searing gout problems rendered them half-sharp or pathologically vicious.

> ALASTAIR DOWN recalling the halcyon days of Stewarding *Weekender* 23 April 1994

I seldom speak to jockeys, because it is irrational to speak to them in one breath, and shout at them in the next.

> The then official Starter, ALEC MARSH *Tote Racing Annual* 1965, J.A. Allen

Starting is rather like driving a car. Just as, with the right timing, it is possible to overtake six cars at once, so with keen anticipation, one should eventually catch all the horses facing the right way simultaneously. No use panicking or losing one's temper. It all hinges on timing.

> I wonder if Keith Brown, alias Captain Cock-Up, had these words, uttered by Jockey Club Starter ALEC MARSH in the 1965 *Tote Racing Annual*, framed and hung on his wall after the 1993 non-National?

Our Hamilton entry Best Of All was pencilled in for the maiden auction restricted to yearlings sold for not more than 5000 guineas. He was sold at Goffs in Ireland for 5000 Irish punts in what turns out to be the only year in living memory that the punt had been stronger than the pound. The result is that our horse is unqualified by a few pence and I'm in trouble with Weatherby's.

> JACK BERRY on why trainers must now be currency exchange experts as well *Weekender* 28 May 1994

INJURY AND RISK

You've got to pretend

You've got to pretend everything's fine. No trainer wants a jockey who isn't 100 per cent fit.

> CARL LLEWELLYN, who has broken his arm, wrist, jaw, cheekbone, ribs and nose – this latter on seven occasions *TV Times* 2-8 April 1994

If you thought about falling you'd be a gibbering wreck.

> Jump jockey LUKE HARVEY *Fit to Ride*, Channel 4, 4 April 1994

If someone told me to climb a mountain in Mongolia to find some snow to put on my leg I'd do it if I thought it would help out in battling back from injury.

> RICHARD GUEST on the lengths a jock will go to for a ride. *Fit to Ride*, Channel 4, 4 April 1994

He got a pretty severe kicking but he couldn't wait to get back into the weighing-room to hear the end of the joke.

> STEVE SMITH ECCLES explaining to the racing media in April 1986 how he had been telling fellow jockey Jonjo O'Neill a risqué yarn when the latter had parted company from his mount in the Cheltenham race

Owners and trainers are worried if there is the slightest thing wrong with their horse, but the jockey is expected to turn up an hour before racing and be 100 per cent fit six days a week for the whole season . . . A horse is allowed to have an off-day, but not a jockey because he runs the risk of losing his livelihood.

> DR MICHAEL TURNER, Jockey Club medical adviser *Racing Post* 19 May 1994

When they've saved your life once they should be discarded.

> Important advice from Jockey Club medical adviser MICHAEL TURNER on the use of helmets *Morning Line*, Channel 4, 7 April 1994

Half a dozen of the flat jockeys in Ireland are wearing what I would call night-shirts rather than body protectors.

Irish Turf Club's medical officer on jockeys unwisely flaunting self-preservation measures Sporting Life *25 May 1994*

The psychology of the jump jockey is far from logical. If you have a long run without a fall you begin to believe it is because of your own talent, yet deep down you know it is inevitable that you will eventually hit the deck.

The longer you go without a fall the nearer the next one comes. It is not a case of shutting it from the mind, but you must trust in the instincts of your mount to survive.

An insight into the jump jockey's dilemma from former champion PETER SCUDAMORE Daily Mail *5 May 1994*

When you are young you are looking for a degree of risk and fun attached. I found it in race riding. Some kids prefer joyriding. I've always felt you could eliminate the danger element to a fair degree, perhaps as much as 80 per cent if you weigh it all up. But if you go head first into everything the dangers are much greater.

DECLAN MURPHY, *quoted by Jonathan Powell* Sunday Express *8 May 1994, shortly before suffering a career-threatening head injury*

On re-licensing injured jockeys: As long as you are strong and fit enough to ride without being a danger to others I have no right to stop you. Complaints like epilepsy or diabetes are different. They can cause a jockey to lose control.

But take a broken femur [thigh] which you might mend by putting a rod inside the bone. If it breaks again, bending the rod, you are in a really serious fix. But provided the jockey has that explained and knows the risk he is running I have no right to stop him riding.

On losing weight quickly: If you sweat off 5 per cent of your weight – say a 120lb man losing 6lb in a sauna – he loses 30 per cent of his strength – we have proved it time and again.

And the extraordinary thing is that jockeys know it themselves. 'I was so weak I could hardly get on the horse', they say – and then expect to feel strong at the end of a three-mile chase.

Jockey Club medical adviser DR MICHAEL TURNER Daily Telegraph *11 October 1993*

If you're going to injure yourself, there are few better places to do it than on a racecourse. Gone are the bad old days when a volunteer with a satchel, trained in little more than mopping up nosebleeds, the treatment of bee stings and coping with the sort of trauma found at village fetes, would be the first on the scene. Tea and sympathy have been replaced by mobile heart monitors, breathing apparatus, pre-loaded injections that save an extra, and possibly vital, five seconds and skilled men who can make instant, life-saving judgements.

MARCUS ARMYTAGE *Daily Telegraph* 9 May 1994

While a jockey is rarely, if ever, frightened, controlled apprehension helps to sharpen the senses and therefore makes riding safer. We all accept the risks we take; nobody goes on to a racecourse believing they are above being injured or, undoubtedly, they will pay the ultimate price. The key to accepting the risks is having an acute will to win. Without that the risks will be perceived as being too great.

JAMIE OSBORNE *The Times* 9 May 1994

Some even suggest running all five- and six-furlong races in lines, similar to athletics.

Unlikely plan to cut down injuries, reported by CLAUD DUVAL *The Sun* 9 May 1994

A dreadful blow

It does a person good to be on death's door. Fate caused the accident and I trust fate will put me back in the saddle.

Recently injured DECLAN MURPHY, quoted by Rachel Murphy in the *Daily Mirror* 20 May 1994

Who is Prime Minister?

Poor Declan Murphy must have felt he was being asked a trick question when his surgeon used this query to check whether he was alert as he recovered from the surgery which saved his life after a dreadful fall. Given the tenuous state of Mr Major's hold on the political scene at the time, Declan could well have inadvertently given the wrong answer! *Daily Mail* 19 May 1994

It does a person good to be at death's door

We all spend every day racing round going about our business. When something like this happens you ask yourself why. This has shown me the value of life and makes things you would normally worry about very small-fry.

> DECLAN MURPHY, recovering from his life-threatening fall at Haydock in May *Racing Post* 19 May 1994

If Declan Murphy's accident had happened at Southwell they would have closed the racecourse immediately.

> Trainer JIMMY HARRIS objecting to the decision to stop all-weather hurdling, referring to the terrible head injuries suffered by Declan Murphy at Haydock *Sporting Life* 4 April 1994

The doctors say he won't be able to ride for a year, so he'll have plenty of time to think things over. I wouldn't care if he chose never to sit on a horse again. The important thing is that he is well and enjoying himself again.

> Girlfriend JO PARK, as Declan Murphy, the jump jockey, recovered from his serious fall from Arcot *Sporting Life* 11 May 1994

I am very fortunate to have only sustained soreness with burns around my neck and chin.

> Relieved amateur PHILIP PRITCHARD who was almost hanged when caught around the neck and dragged off his mount at Cheltenham by the infamous grey gate tape, responsible for the 1993 Aintree fiasco as it malfunctioned on its final appearance at the track *Racing Post* 19 May 1994

One year at Cheltenham I fell and a horse stood on my face. I was cut open from my eyebrow to the tip of my nose. At the hospital the surgeon asked Mary [his wife] if she'd like to see the inside of a nose. I had 32 stitches. That was on the Wednesday and I rode a winner on the Friday.

> DICK FRANCIS *Today* 9 April 1994

His death has united men, women and children in grief all over the country who had ever heard of him. Horses are the connecting link that binds that wide fellowship.

All members of it felt a dreadful blow when the news came from Lingfield. Race meetings, shows, gymkhanas and point-to-points have shown their respects. Bookmakers stopped shouting, barmaids stopped pouring drinks – the only sound you could hear was the song of birds.

He was a thoroughly nice man, and now we are left to ask why did fate play such a dirty trick on such a man. But Steve was a realist and he knew the risks of his profession.

He ran those risks willingly but that doesn't make his death any easier to bear.

> A moving address by LORD OAKSEY to 250 mourners at the funeral of jockey Steve Wood, tragically killed in a fall at Lingfield at the age of 26, 13 May 1994

It was not the fall itself that did the damage but the blow from another runner. It's the moment when a horse stops being something you shout at in a betting shop and becomes half a ton of heavy-weight with a hammer in its hoof.

> BROUGH SCOTT on the tragic death of Steve Wood *Sunday Times* 8 May 1994

It was one of the fastest races I've ridden in, with half a dozen front-runners. I was near the back and I saw Steve's horse bob and go down, and I had time to snatch round. But those just behind him could do nothing. We flat jockeys are men with boys' frames; the jump riders are men with men's frames. All the body protectors in the world could not have saved Steve, the way the horses galloped over him and kicked him.

> Harrowing eye-witness account of the accident to Steve Wood, by fellow rider BILLY NEWNES *Independent on Sunday* 9 May 1994

SUPERSTITIONS

I don't like to

I don't like to bet on my own horses; it seems to jinx them. I just don't know how they find out I'm betting, when they are in the post parade.

> Englishman training in the USA JONATHAN SHEPPARD

I won a bunch of races in a row with Owens Troupe one year. The first race he won, I was wearing a white summer suit. I was wearing that suit in the dead of winter at Aqueduct.

> US trainer GARY CONTESSA

Whenever I get into a slump I'll create superstitions, things that you know have nothing to do with the outcome of the race, just things you create in your mind.

> Jockey turned trainer ANGEL CORDERO, Jr

I don't believe in luck, just fast horses.

> LUCA CUMANI

I never like to say 'this horse can't lose', because whenever you say something like that it's sure to lose.

> New York trainer JOHN D. DeSTEFANO, Jr

I don't want to see a hat on a chair or bed.

> New York trainer PHILIP GEORGE JOHNSON

I'm too superstitious to talk about them.

> Breeders' Cup-winning US trainer WILLIAM I. MOTT

I usually wear my underwear inside-out for good luck.

> Panamanian-born jockey LAFFIT PINCAY, Jr

I don't have any. They're bad luck.

> Chilean-born jockey JOSE ADEON SANTOS

Not to speak any more in public, as the last three efforts have resulted in a marriage, a two-year driving ban and a fine for trying to rob friends of the late and unlamented Lord Wigg.

> Former trainer turned owner and the 'brains' behind the Gay Future affair, TONY COLLINS *Sporting Life* 1 June 1994

Never bet on a horse whose name has been changed – he is sure to be unlucky.

> *Dictionary of Omens and Superstitions* Treasure Press, 1978

I suddenly thought, it's all daftness.

> Jump jockey PHIL TUCK, formerly the most superstitious of jockeys, who in 1988 announced he'd decided it was all a waste of time

The local feelings on such matters are very strong.

> Spokesperson for the Royal Hong Kong Jockey Club in September 1992 explaining why they would not grant permission for the widow of former champion jockey there, Noel Barker, to scatter his ashes on Sha Tin racecourse

When I first started training, people were saying don't run in this race or that race because horses who win it never go on to win Classics. But I don't believe in that sort of thing.

> HENRY CECIL (*Sunday Telegraph* October 1993) on superstition – a man who self-confessedly refuses to wear green for superstitious reasons, claiming: 'Most of my family have died in green.' He also once told the *Sporting Life* that he always stopped his car en route to the races to put in petrol, otherwise, 'If I don't fill it up I don't win.'

A horrible pigeon got into my house a few weeks back and made a terrible mess everywhere, including on our heads! I hate it. It's a nightmare but I'm stuck with it. Since I've been in racing I've grown more and more superstitious. Normally I'd have the pigeon killed, but I daren't. I'm sure it would bring us bad luck.

> Trainer SUE BRAMALL *The Sun* 23 April 1994

I'm not a great believer in luck. I walk under ladders all the time.

> ROBERT SANGSTER *Sunday Times* 22 May 1994

THERE'S ONLY ONE LESTER

It's all very strange

You can have 50/1 Glory, Boredom at 7/4 or Money at 1/2.

> Anonymous bookmaker on Lester's reason for coming back. Quoted by Colin Fleetwood-Jones, Ruff's Guide to the Turf 1991 *Sporting Life*

I think Lester's potty! What on earth does he think he's doing? It's all very strange – it surprises me immensely.

> LORD HOWARD DE WALDEN on Lester's comeback, Ruff's Guide to the Turf 1991 *Sporting Life*

His name doesn't have the pulling power that it used to have.

> A seriously miffed PHILIP JOHNSTON of the Royal Hong Kong Jockey Club who withdrew Lester's licence to ride there after he did the unforgivable and went to ride in Macau. One wonders whether Hong Kong or Lester was the real sufferer from this decision, reported by the *Daily Telegraph* 2 April 1994

Lester, if you do that to me again, I'll put my foot so far up your backside it will take me a week to get it out.

> SCOBIE BREASLEY in the *Sporting Life* 1993, recalling a pleasant, if one-sided, conversation he had with an early 1950s Lester at Newbury

I've got nothing against Lester, but I think I'm on a winner.

> Overweight, lumbago-suffering hospital gardener TREVOR THOMAS of Swansea who in 1993 bet a tenner at 5/1 (with Hills) that he would outlive the Long Fellow. They are both 58.

One of the grandest sights in racing has always been to see Lester hauled before the stewards. He goes in there like Clint Eastwood and he comes out like Clint Eastwood. Lester doesn't give a monkey's.

Jockey BRYN CROSSLEY *The Guardian* 6 November 1993

When Lester won the St Leger on Ribocco, I had the whole week's wages on him and as I walked towards the betting shop afterwards I heard someone saying 'effing Piggott'. The suspense before I found out whether Piggott was effing for losing the race or effing for beating that punter's horse was almost unbearable.

> Comedy actor ENN REITEL in 1988, having also admitted that he used to back horses tipped by clairvoyant Maurice Woodruff – but psychic readers knew that already

Not bad, was it?

> LESTER PIGGOTT after riding a double in Dubai – his first winners since breaking a collarbone in a Breeders' Cup fall in February 1993

Don't be —ing silly. I've got to go out there and earn my £14 riding fee in the next race.

> LESTER's reported remark to the course doctor who wanted him to rest after taking a tumble on Irish Derby Day 1977

We British have an almost insane desire to make heroes of people who knock the system, and tax evasion always figures large in this category. What everyone should remember is that when he cheated the Inland Revenue, Lester Piggott effectively stole from every man, woman and child in this country.

It is true that Piggott served time in prison for his crime but it cannot be argued that he has paid his debt to society.

> So, do you think it is unlikely that *Racing Post* letter-writer MICHAEL HAKEN of Halifax will bother to dig into his pocket to help finance the statue of tribute to the Long Fellow being suggested by some correspondents? 10 May 1994

Has the undoubted magic of the inimitable Lester Piggott lost its glitter? I pose the question because the great man's offers to ride in the 2000 Guineas have been met with stark indifference from trainers so far.

> COLIN MACKENZIE – writing LP off too soon? *Daily Mail* 21 April 1994

The old jockeys used to say you could not be sure of riding your horse in the Derby until you reached the start. Then you knew Lester would not be climbing on it.

> WILLIE CARSON *Sunday Express* 24 April 1994

Far too old

His career is over, he's 55 and that's far too old to be rushing up and down the country trying to get rides.

> Ill-considered welcome back to Lester from colleague WILLIE CARSON as the comeback got under way

It's still the same. One leg each side.

> LESTER PIGGOTT's reported answer to a questioner wondering how he would find racing on his comeback

His career is over, he's 55 and that's far too old

How sad and ironic that on Derby Day Lester Piggott, who was jailed for tax evasion, should be cold-shouldered by the Queen, who does not pay tax at all.

> Letter to the *Daily Mirror* June 1991

The fact that the maestro has ridden 30 Classic winners has to be all the proof needed for awarding the Queen's ultimate accolade, a knighthood, for outstanding dedication to thoroughbred horseracing for almost 40 years.

> Letter from TOMAS FOXX-FOY of Cardiff in the *Racing Post* 20 April 1994.

If Lester Piggott's net horseracing fortune is £13 million, it must have been a dizzy sum before he handed over a fat slice to the Inland Revenue.

> JOE JOSEPH commenting on a wealth survey which made Lester the sixth-richest sportsman in Britain *The Times* 29 April 1994

My biggest failure as a trainer – I never made a gentleman of Lester Piggott.

> Trainer JACK JARVIS's oft-repeated remark from the mid-1950s *The Flat*, Roger Mortimer, George Allen & Unwin, 1979

They had taken notice of his dangerous and erratic riding both this season and in previous seasons, and that in spite of continuous warnings, he continued to show complete disregard for the Rules of Racing and for the safety of other jockeys.

> Message from the STEWARDS OF THE JOCKEY CLUB for young jockey Lester, issued in 1954 after an incident at Royal Ascot. He was out until 1955 after being suspended for six months

I believe now there is a case for having two [jockey] championships – one which starts on 1 January and ends on 31 December, and another for the traditional flat season.

> LESTER PIGGOTT *Mail on Sunday* April 1994. Oh yes, Lester – and what about another championship for jockeys without private planes or helicopters to get them from meeting to meeting, or another for jockeys who only feel like riding when there's an 'R' in the month or when the temperature is above 62 degrees?

I'd rather have a cheque.

> LESTER PIGGOTT, having been offered 'a most attractive Brazilian stone set of ashtrays' by grateful owner ROBERT ELLIS, having partnered his Pirate Way to a 100/8 victory at Nottingham *Sporting Life* 21 May 1994

CELEBRITY COMMENTS

Playing the horses

Telly... loved playing the horses. He would join the strong Greek Cypriot gang in the shop [William Hill, Park Lane, London] and seldom left a race alone, horses or greyhounds.

> CHARLES BENSON recalling the betting habits of recently deceased actor Telly Savalas *Sunday Express* 30 January 1994

An adult Christmas.

> STUART BARNES, England rugby union international, on the delights of the Cheltenham Festival *The Independent* 15 March 1994

I was on the rough side with a coach party and knew Harry [Carr] well. As he turned to go down after the parade, he noticed me in the crowd, pointed to his horse [Parthia] and stuck a thumb up.

> England international cricketer DENIS COMPTON revealing how he – and the rest of his coach party – backed the 10/1 winner of the 1959 Derby

It is certain that they won't allow me to help you become rich, just as it was always a certainty that Ned Sherrin would never let me play me even for one lousy night.

> Racing writer and low-life specialist JEFFREY BERNARD reflecting on the fact that the play 'Jeffrey Bernard is Unwell', based on his life, was to feature a daily racing tip (not from him) and also that he wasn't deemed talented enough to portray himself in the play *The Spectator* 8 January 1994

It's hard to describe the feeling. It was one of supreme bliss, ecstasy. It was like watching your daughter running in a real race and winning after being in diapers.

> STANLEY (aka rapper MC Hammer) BURRELL after his Lite Light won the 1991 American Oaks *NYRA Media Guide* 1993

Coming racing is a relaxation – in football it is high tension.

> England and Manchester United star BRYAN ROBSON at Chester, where the high tension was relieved by a winning tip from Old Trafford fan Walter Swinburn on whose advice the United squad had risked a large proportion of their win bonus for landing the Premiership title, on Cicerao, which won at 2/1 *Sporting Life* 6 May 1994

I have the man who keeps me alive to thank for making me back Dallas.

> Film star WALTER MATTHAU explaining to TV viewers following the 1986 William Hill Cambridgeshire that his heart surgeon R.B. Chesne had tipped him the winner

If I go to the races with £100 in my pocket and come back with £99 I've had a good day. If I end up with £101 I've had an excellent day.

> Actor FRAZER HINES *Weekender* 2 April 1994

The last horse I backed was Tulyar.

> Former MP turned TV interrogator BRIAN WALDEN, claiming to have been betless since supporting the 1952 Derby winner *Morning Line*, Channel 4, 14 May 1994

I might put it on a horse. I've never had a bet on a horse in my entire life but I would go round to John McCririck, the Channel 4 racing presenter, for his recommendation. If it won I would buy *Punch* magazine and employ lots of wonderful cartoonists.

> Launching a 'Win £30,000' promotion, the *Independent on Sunday* asked writer and broadcaster LIBBY PURVES, presenter of Radio 4's *Midweek*, how she might spend that amount

He was my great hero, a model figure of what I thought a Corinthian amateur jockey should be.

> THE HON. NICHOLAS SOAMES, MP paying tribute to Lord Oaksey *Horse and Hound* 12 May 1994

Ups and downs

The ups are fantastic and the downs don't get any easier.

> MADELEINE, wife of Sir Andrew Lloyd Webber, after Raymylette became her first winner as an owner just 48 hours after her Joe Gillis had collapsed and died at Kempton *Sporting Life* 25 January 1994

All the lads who work for me are Manchester United fans

He is my favourite horse. Not just because he's a winner but because he's a survivor – a bit like Bet in the 'Street'.

> JULIE GOODYEAR, alias Bet Lynch, on Red Rum *The Sun* 23 April 1994

All the lads who work for me are Manchester United fans. They have been sneering and crowing about United every morning when we go out to work the horses. If we win at Old Trafford, I don't think they will turn in on Monday. It will be a good excuse to sack the lot of them! Imagine going to an industrial tribunal and saying you sacked people for being United fans? Surely that's a good enough reason.

> Trainer and Chairman of Manchester City, FRANCIS LEE, contemplating revenge on his disloyal stable lads with respect to a 'derby' game with United which, sadly for Franny, City lost 2-0 *The Star* 23 April 1994

was black and blue so often I decided those colours would be fine.

> Former Irish premier CHARLES HAUGHEY, explaining how his experience of hunting mishaps led to his choice of racing colours *Racing Post* 17 March 1994

I had three horses in training and to be honest they were virtually bankrupting me. Every time I turned around there seemed to be another bill and eventually I realised it was a mug's game. So the horses have been sold and I've gone back to fishing. It's quieter and cheaper.

ERIC CLAPTON, April 1986

There is no better feeling in sport than seeing your own horse win.

Slightly surprising declaration from former Olympic gold medallist JOHN WALKER, the flying Kiwi who has established himself as a leading owner/breeder in his native land *Daily Mail* 7 May 1994

I think it's harder to come up with a big horse.

85-year-old film-maker CUBBY BROCCOLI asked to compare the thrill of producing a blockbuster movie with that of owning Santa Anita Derby winner Brocco *Racing Post* 13 April 1994

Freddie told me to go up to 50,000 guineas, but I said if I'm going to spend that kind of money you'd better see what you're getting, so he came to the sale. I started bidding on him, but then Freddie took over, sticking his tongue out at the auctioneer.

Trainer OWEN BRENNAN on how his owner Freddie Starr purchased Grand National winner-to-be Miinnehoma at the Doncaster Spring Sales *Pacemaker & Thoroughbred Breeder* May 1994

I keep reading that I could earn £400,000 – but to do that we would have to win the League, the Cup, the Boat Race and the Grand National.

Then Norwich manager MIKE WALKER on efforts to keep him at the club *The Independent* 6 January 1994

Getting any money out of Michael Fish is virtually impossible. I would love to have a horse, but it would mean about a dozen of us putting in around a thousand pounds apiece.

TV weatherman JOHN KETTLEY on the difficulties of persuading his fellow meteorologists of the wisdom of ownership *Racing Post* 8 April 1994

It was Lady Joseph's idea; she asked me if it was a gelding and she said: 'Oh let's call it Mister Bobbit.' We knocked off the 't' to make sure it got through.

CHARLIE BROOKS on how owner Lady Joseph, 71, came to name a horse after the man whose penis was severed by his unhappy wife.

I haven't ridden for 20 years, but being a part of the Grand National fired up my enthusiasm again. So I'll get myself a young jumper and go for it. If everything goes to plan I could be entering races by next year. Who knows, I might even ride in the National one day.

> Yes, and hamsters might be eaten by comedians! Highly unlikely *News of the World* story about FREDDIE STARR, owner of Miinnehoma, 17 April 1994

Wrapped up in racing

I became completely wrapped up in racing. I get all the papers and magazines and read up on every horse going. It's always been in my blood but it really gripped me once I became an owner.

> Soccer star and Irish international NIALL QUINN, then of Manchester City, *The People* October 1993

I've played in big matches – Wembley internationals, World Cup games – and I never, ever happen to have been as nervous as I was before Cois Na Tine's first race. I was shaking like a leaf.

> NIALL QUINN of Manchester City and Republic of Ireland on the horse he later sold for a reported £250,000 (*Raceform Update* 23 April 1994). He explained why he chose to sell: 'I would have had to win about five League Championships and three European Cups to earn the same money. It was put to me that by refusing the offer it would have been like putting on forty or fifty thousand pounds to win, every time it ran, should it fail in the future.'

Stanley had a clause inserted into his contract which said the chairman should provide him with a winner a week while he was at the club.

> Trainer REG HOLLINSHEAD who attended the contract signing when Stanley Matthews signed for Stoke City, whose chairman, Gordon Taylor, was one of Reg's owners *Sporting Life* 20 May 1994

A marvellous achievement. Broadway Flyer was the first South African-bred winner ever in England and now he's won the Vase. Thanks a million. Gary Player.

> Fax message to trainer John Hills from the veteran golf-ace GARY PLAYER who bred the 1994 Chester Vase winner Broadway Flyer *The Sun* 7 May 1994

People ask me whether I would rather win the Derby or the British Open. I tell them that I'd rather win the Epsom Derby than two British Opens.

> GARY PLAYER, who sold Broadway Flyer for $45,000 but flew over to watch it compete in the 1994 Derby *Daily Telegraph* 27 May 1994

It was like being a slave.

> FRANK MALONEY, manager of Lennox Lewis, remembering his three-week stint as a stable lad in Epsom *Daily Telegraph* 10 November 1993

My aim was to ride as an amateur eventually. I don't think I would have kept Fred Winter awake at night.

> Frustrated jockey turned actor/racecourse commentator MILTON JOHNS, alias *Coronation Street*'s deceased corner-shop owner Brendan Scott *Sporting Life* November 1993

Breakfast was a Kit-Kat.

> Equestrian star LUCINDA GREEN on a day spent with exiled trainer Michael Dickinson in Maryland *Daily Telegraph* 8 December 1993

I find it all quite relaxing and really enjoy helping out. I'm not afraid to get my hands dirty.

> Unemployed soccer boss BOBBY GOULD, helping out at trainer Pat Murphy's stables. Gould is part owner of filly Homemaker *Daily Mail* November 1993

My grandad was a corner-end bookie – there were no betting shops in those days, so if you wanted to bet you went to the bookie at the end of the street. My grandparents had a bowl full of silver. The money would go in there and he'd pay out the bets with it. When I was about seven my mother said, 'Never take anything out of there,' and I said, 'I never have, mother, and I never will.' Well, I never did after that, but it was a lie because I had taken sixpence out once before.

> JACK CHARLTON *Telegraph Magazine* 28 May 1994

I could tell he had bet too much trying to get out. He walked past me, not knowing where he was. I watched him. He walked right into the women's crapper. They screamed and he came running out. It pulled him out and he caught the winner of the next race. But I would not advise this system to all losers.

> From *Another Horse Story* by US writer CHARLES BUKOWSKI (died March 1994, aged 73)

ABROAD

Local meetings

Searching for information about the local meetings can be an interesting exercise which qualifies you for an award from both MENSA and the Sherlock Holmes Appreciation Society.

> TONY and SHARON SLAUGHTER *Go Racing in France*, 1994, discussing regional newspaper coverage of racing

The big race favourite walks to the track through the traffic, led behind a bicycle; the oldest jockey riding is a fresh-faced 22; the bottom weight in the fourth race carries four and a half stone; and the only bet allowed is a straight forecast.

> ALASTAIR OSBORNE, on a typical day's racing at Ho Chi Minh City's track *The Independent* 24 May 1994

In keeping with their government's track record of insisting that night is frequently day, betting on horseracing has been deemed 'fun' not gambling.

> RONALD ATKIN explaining how in China, where gambling is banned, betting is permitted at Guangzhou racetrack *Sunday Telegraph* 10 April 1994

The frocks on display then, worn as only French women can wear them, tend to make Royal Ascot look like a grunge party.

> SUE MONTGOMERY on Chantilly on French Derby Day *Independent on Sunday* 6 June 1994

In the northern hemisphere's off-season, Hong Kong provides the highest standard of riding anywhere in the world. You have to be the best, you won't get away with anything less. A jockey as good as Dean McKeown couldn't crack it here and went back to Britain early. Lester Piggott cut short his stay this year, too.

> ROBIN PARKE, racing correspondent of the *South China Morning Post*, reported by Ronald Atkin *Sunday Telegraph* 10 April 1994

French women tend to make Royal Ascot look like a grunge party

The racetrack is the barometer of the situation. If it is open, people know that times are good.

> DR GHAZI YEHYA, official vet at Hippodrome racecourse, Beirut, which, since the civil war began in 1975, had been closed except for spells during 1976 and 1978 until it reopened in 1993 *Sunday Express* magazine, 13 March 1994

Today, in the melting pot that is the new South Africa, racing is fully economically driven, without racial or other constraints. There are black, coloured, white and Indian owners, bookmakers, trainers and jockeys – and, yes, even female apprentices at the national jockeys academy.

> KAREL MIEDEMA on the state of South African racing *Pacemaker & Thoroughbred Breeder* June 1994

As soon as a horse got beat, you were the first to be blamed and you were on your way. There are few regulations and it is a little crooked.

> STEVE DAWSON, returning from riding in Mauritius where there is a high turnover of jockeys *Sporting Life* 1 December 1993

Arc Day is really very ordinary.

> Epsom Managing Director TIM NELIGAN *Sporting Life* 31 May 1994

Here, most jockeys have some sort of retainer and in general they have more security, so the weighing-room atmosphere is much more relaxed.

> German-based jockey MARK RIMMER *Pacemaker & Thoroughbred Breeder* March 1994

The best thing about Fort Erie is the people. If you have a winner, everyone is delighted. At Woodbine, they're more likely to try to steal your owner.

> Englishman EDWARD FREEMAN, training at Fort Erie, Canada, 1993

Over here racing is considered immoral. When an MP becomes a Minister, he sells his racehorse.

> JANET SLADE of *Paris Turf* quoted by Peter Scudamore *Daily Mail* 7 April 1994

Khruschev used to say 'We don't need horses; we need tractors.'

> BAZARBAY MEREDOV, deputy director of Ashkhabad horse farm in newly independent Turkmenistan, explaining how the old society rule depleted the local Akhal Tekke racehorses *The Observer* 8 May 1994

If you pay a jockey US$100 to stop a horse, he'll stop it. That's a fortune to a farmer's son. You can ban him for life, he won't care.

> TRAN YAN NGHIA, vice-director of Ho Chi Minh City's Phutto Sport Club, which runs racing there, explaining why it is not wise to risk one's shirt on a hot favourite at the track. Quoted byAlastair Osborne in *The Independent* 25 May 1994

The main difference is the law. You can get a good beer, meal, watch large screens, play fruit machines, open when you like – even Sundays.

> ANDY SELBY, Wolverhampton man who had been working in betting shops in Prague and Slovenia for two years *Racing Post* 22 April 1994

Let's face it, there's bugger all for the man in the street to do over there. It's virgin territory for the leisure industry.

> SIS Regional Manager International, TONY DOGHERTY, as the service opened up in a Russian betting shop *Sporting Life* 20 April 1994

We had the form from the English papers up on the wall and they didn't need the help of the translators we had laid on. They picked it up right away. Can you imagine the scene in the average shop over here if we stuck a Russian form up on the wall. They're what I would call brain-active.

> LIAM CASHMAN on the Plus Minus betting shop he is involved with in St Petersburg *Sporting Life* 20 April 1994

Jockeys must expect criticism, so long as the facts are truly stated and comment does not convey imputations of an evil sort.

> The judge who dismissed Kiwi jockey G. Barclay's claim for £500 damages after the *Evening Star* newspaper criticised his riding in 1936

It is my belief that a German-trained horse will come to Epsom with a real chance before the year 2000.

> JULIAN MUSCAT on where he thinks the next power in racing will emerge *Weekender* 8 January 1994

Don't believe all you read about Japan and how their racing is the Promised Land. It is achieved at a price unacceptable to societies with a history of democratic institutions.

> JOHN McCRIRICK, after attending the tenth Japan Cup *Racing Post* 3 December 1993

I could have won, but I don't know. I am just in a panic. I feel very ashamed. I made a big mistake.

> Understatement, perhaps, from jockey KENT DESORMEAUX who mistook the winning post and dropped his hands too early, losing the world's richest race, the Japan Cup, on Kotashaan. Still, only 179,619 were watching him *Sporting Life* 29 November 1993

I'm going to miss you Malcolm, our chats over the year have been most enlightening.

> Chief Steward at Randwick, Australia, JOHN SCHRECK to retiring jockey Malcolm Johnston in September 1993, the latter having been suspended on 56 occasions in his 32-year career

Cable network sports was no use at all when it came to finding coverage of the Grand National. I spent a fruitless Saturday scouring the whole of Barbados in my effort to witness the happenings at Aintree. Now I realise my mistake – I wanted to see an event that was important and had nothing to do with cricket. Silly me

> *Daily Telegraph*'s 'Talking Sport' writer KATE BATTERSBY on the difficulties of following racing from the West Indies, 12 April 1994

Treated like pop stars

The jockeys get treated like pop stars.

> Alan Munro's Business Manager, MAURICE HALE, on racing in Hong Kong
> *Sporting Life* 1 December 1993

If I went into a restaurant with Robert Redford and there was one seat left, he'd be left on his feet.

> DEAN MCKEOWN on the perks of riding in Hong Kong, adding: 'Their theory is that they have to pay to see a film star, but we can give them a tip and they can get money out of us.'

It is a very fickle place for both trainers and jockeys. If you don't click very early on, you're out.

> Brit trainer in Hong Kong DAVID OUGHTON *Pacemaker & Thoroughbred Breeder* April 1994

Another ten minutes and I would have been gone, that is a certainty. But I was back at the racecourse supervising the training of my horses two weeks later.

> Top trainer in Hong Kong IVAN ALLAN, recalling how prompt action saved his life when in Singapore in 1984 he was shot four times at close range by a gunman – fortunately not a major problem thus far in the streets of Lambourn or Newmarket *Daily Telegraph* 25 May 1994

Drinking in the afternoon

The Irish feel no guilt about gambling, or drinking in the afternoon; perhaps that is where our two nations differ most and if there are Irish who don't care for a gamble or a slug of paddy's, they don't go racing, they stay at home.

> CLEMENT FREUD *Sporting Life* 11 March 1994

If the politicians of the two parts of the country behaved to one another with the same bonhomie as the racing folk, there would be no troubles.

> CLEMENT FREUD on Ireland *Sporting Life* 11 March 1994

A straw poll among regulars at Tipperary and Naas revealed 33 per cent who knew what the figures meant. A further 28 per cent had not the foggiest, 22 per cent thought it was some sort of rating system and 17 per cent said it referred to the number of days since the horse last ran.

> MICHAEL CLOWER, report from Ireland *Sporting Life* 20 March 1994. And just what *were* the mysterious figures which had appeared on the racecards at these courses? The weight carried by each horse – in pounds.

Cash used to get terrible stick from a section of Irish punters. They love to hassle foreign jockeys. I don't know whether it is false patriotism, but when things don't work out for visiting jockeys they get a lot of criticism, much of it unfair.

> Top Irish trainer JOHN OXX using Cash Asmussen to explain the Irish treatment of star jockeys from abroad *Racing Post* 12 May 1994

The idea that the popularity of racing could dwindle to the point of extinction is a shocking one, but there are precedents.

> Warning to Irish racing by STEWART KENNY, Managing Director of bookies Paddy Power, citing the example of hurling's decline *Racing Post* 27 April 1994

The idea that racing (the Irish version as seen here at the Curragh) could dwindle to the point of extinction is a shocking one

A conveniently sited mosque

Free admission, free racecards, no betting and a conveniently sited mosque adjacent to the furlong pole.

RICHARD EVANS on racing at Jebel Ali, Dubai *The Times* 25 March 1994

Then there is betting. Currently it is illegal, but in this most westernised of Arab countries you would not wager your last dirham on it staying that way.

RICHARD EVANS on Dubai *The Times* 25 March 1994

The sport cannot be progressing quicker anywhere else on this planet. Starting from dust in the desert barely four years ago Dubai now has two modern racecourses.

RICHARD EDMONDSON on Dubai *The Independent* 25 March 1994

The sight of racegoers rubbing noses as they greeted each other may not be normal practice in Britain, but some racing traditions clearly cross international boundaries. The official starter wore a bowler hat.

RICHARD EVANS on racing in Dubai *The Times* 26 March 1994

The idea of racing came from here in the first place, and the thoroughbred in Europe evolved from stallions from this area. I remember once someone asked me, 'Why do you like racing?' I answered: 'We started it!'

SHEIKH MOHAMMED, the world's biggest owner, interviewed in Dubai by Tony Stafford *Daily Telegraph* 29 March 1994

At the moment the racing has a strange feel of boys with their train sets, as small fields of family-owned competitors take each other on. This may be as it was in Britain 200 years ago when noblemen and their entourages filed into a field to pit their best horses against one another.

RICHARD EDMONDSON on racing in Dubai, *The Independent* 1 April 1994

The Melbourne Cup 1993

This is probably the furthest anyone has brought a racehorse to win a race.

DERMOT WELD, Irish trainer of winner Vintage Crop

I think we'll soon be seeing Australian horses coming to Europe to have a go at races like the King George, and the Arc.

DERMOT WELD

Much of the credit for his [Vintage Crop's] trouble-free journey must be down to the insect-free jet stall which we used for the very first time.

MICHAEL DOWLING of the BBA (Ireland) who organised travel arrangements

The final frontier was breached when Vintage Crop ushered in a new era of racing as a global sport.

RICHARD EDMONDSON *The Independent*

You are now part of Australia's racing history.

DAVID BOURKE, Chairman of the Victoria Racing Club, to winning connections

This will become a race that every decent stayer in Europe will want to contest.

Vintage Crop's owner DR MICHAEL SMURFIT

It just goes to show that the Irish can do anything.

Previous Cup-winning trainer BART CUMMINGS

Jeez, we gave those Poms a 200-year start. Now we are 100 years ahead of them.

Nine times Melbourne Cup-winning trainer BART CUMMINGS in 1992

Go racing in Melbourne during the Cup and you will experience a vibrancy which is sadly lacking at Royal Ascot, the Newmarket July meeting, Epsom and too many other big fixtures.

RICHARD EVANS *The Times* October 1993

It could have been worse – the Pommie horse might have won.

Anonymous Aussie racegoer immediately after Vintage Crop from Ireland had become the first non Aussie or Kiwi based winner of the Melbourne Cup, in 1993, with England's Drum Taps ninth.

**Go racing in Melbourne during the Cup and you will
experience a vibrancy which is sadly lacking at Royal Ascot**

In a Melbourne Cup the first nine furlongs are usually OK, but the
remaining seven can be pretty rough. At around the seven, everyone starts jockeying for the best positions and the visitors will be
done no favours. The local jockeys would figure they will probably
never see them again anyway.

> Aussie-born jockey GEORGE MOORE on the reception foreign riders
> contesting the Cup can expect. Nonetheless, in 1993 Vintage Crop from
> Ireland put the locals to shame with a great victory for trainer Dermot
> Weld and jockey Michael Kinane.

Irish racing is basking in your glory.

> Fax to Dermot Weld from the Stewards of the Turf Club

A champion horse, a champion trainer and a champion jockey.

> Aussie trainer LEE FREEDMAN on Vintage Crop's connections

I think the Australian owner and trainer will find it hard to win the
Melbourne Cup in the future.

> Aussie trainer JOHN MEAGHER

The Australians were a pretty sorry lot after this, and collective recrimination and self-flagellation were the order of the post-race week.

> How the Aussies reacted to Vintage Crop's Melbourne Cup defeat of their finest *Highflyer International* 1993, Vol. 21, Issue 3

The jump races are started out of stalls and the standard of stewarding is much stricter than over here.

> PETER SCUDAMORE on racing in Australia *Daily Mail* 21 May 1994

Speed, speed and more speed

Our racing is about three things – speed, speed and more speed. If you've got that, it doesn't really matter where you're drawn.

> US trainer JOHN VEITCH *Daily Express* November 1993

I think that drug abuse in stables is more rampant than it ever was. From 1989 to the present it has got worse. The horse owner is pressing the trainer to win at any cost.

> US vet DR GREGORY FERRARO *Sports Illustrated* October 1993

Horseracing has all but disappeared in America.

> FRANK D. FORDE, former editor of *Sports Illustrated* on BBC Radio 5, 3 February 1994

OTB [New York's Off Track Betting Corporation] actually lost a million dollars for the fiscal year which ended on 30 June, an astonishing achievement considering the fact that it is a Parimutuel operation with a built-in take-out of at least 22 per cent on every dollar.

> ALAN SHUBACK *Sporting Life* 26 November 1993

He's fourth, Mrs Genter, he's third, Mrs Genter . . . he's second, Mrs Genter, he's taking the lead, Mrs Genter, he's a winner, he's a winner, you've won the Kentucky Derby, Mrs Genter. I love you, Mrs Genter.

> No, not Mr Genter, but trainer CARL NAFZGER's widely reported 'commentary' on the 1990 Kentucky Derby for the 92-year-old, wheelchair-bound owner of winner Unbridled

The Americans don't support our racing; why should we back theirs?

> ALEC STEWART explaining why his Mtoto would not be contesting the 1988 Breeders' Cup *Sporting Life* July 1988

Newspaper coverage of horseracing in most areas outside of New York is pathetic. Even in Kentucky it's unsatisfactory. Television coverage is spotty at best, and the commentators with a few notable exceptions are usually so offensive or so ignorant that they ruin the broadcast. The public has no idea who the horses are any more and is held hostage to whatever the media releases to them.

> The state of media coverage of racing in the USA by 'Fair Play' of *Highflyer International*, Vol. 2, Issue 2, 1993. Perhaps we should send them Thommo, the *Daily Sport* and our own version of the Big Mac!

The Breeders' Cup 1993

It is Mickey Mouse racing for megabucks . . . boring to read about and even more boring to watch.

> *Sporting Life* reader CHRIS RICKETT's opinion of the Breeders' Cup.

I don't even know how to pronounce the horse's name.

> JERRY BAILEY, rider of shock 133/1 French-horse Breeders' Cup Classic winner Arcangues

I'm not very good at quotes.

> First female Breeders' Cup-winning jockey BLYTHE MILLER, who won the chase on Lonesome Glory

It's a dangerous race. They were bloody lucky there was no disaster.

> Trainer JOHN GOSDEN after the Breeders' Cup Mile

He was kind of flopping about.

> US jockey JERRY BAILEY describing Walter Swinburn's riding style in the Breeders' Cup

My wife was shaking so hard, we left the track right away.

> Anonymous Breeders' Cup punter who won $1.6 million on a Breeders' Cup accumulator after picking Arcangues by accident

In recent years the feeling was that we no longer needed the race to stimulate interest in the other races.

> Breeders' Cup Director D.G. VAN CLIEF on the demise of the Breeders' Cup Chase, 7 March 1994

The cynics call it the Bleeders' Cup.

> TIM RICHARDS *Benson & Hedges Racing Year* Pelham Books, 1989

Fair Play is so sick of Breeders' Cup dictating the championships. She can't believe that its originators intended to reduce an entire season of racing to one single day in November. Why is racing on the decline? Perhaps because its own people have supported the idea that you don't have to follow racing but for one day of the year, when they award the championships in the Breeders' Cup winner's circles. Why should anyone be interested in a graded stakes in May or June? Why should we care about the Triple Crown at all, if it's all thrown out the window in November?

> Not everyone loves the Breeders' Cup – even in the States – as this critical comment by 'Fair Play' in *Highflyer International*, Vol. 2, 1994, demonstrated

COME AGAIN?

High behind

I got cold feet when I saw her in the parade ring. She's still high behind.

> Trainer MARK JOHNSTON on winning filly Millstream *Racing Post* 11 May 1994

Danoli is too good for me to say how good he is.

> Trainer TOM FOLEY after his horse won at Cheltenham *Daily Telegraph* 17 March 1993

Susan knocks off Johnnie on St Valentines Day.

> Dubious-looking *Sporting Life* headline from 1987. The truth was less lurid – Sue Bradburne, wife of jockey Johnnie, was competing alongside him in a hunter class when her horse veered across to bump his, knocking him clean out of the saddle.

Mr Dunlop didn't like him last year – thought he was just a horse.

> WILLIE CARSON on Erhaab *Sporting Life* 12 May 1994

Almost as soon as he came to us he got a bit of a leg . . . and then he went a bit wrong behind.

> Let's hope he's got the other three legs and turned himself the right way round by now, then! NICKY HENDERSON on Lingfield winner Sesame Seed *Racing Post* 21 March 1994

He couldn't have been himself last time.

> MARTIN PIPE on General Mouktar *Racing Post* 14 March 1994

He's a lazy bastard. He doesn't jump properly and he doesn't travel.

> Highly complimentary comments by jockey DAVID BRIDGWATER after riding Grange Brake at Cheltenham – after, believe it or not, they'd won! *Racing Post* 21 April 1994

If it was [good to soft going] then my bum is a bloater.

> STEVE WOODMAN, slightly sceptical about Kempton's going after his King Credo disappointed *Sporting Life* 1 January 1994

We've had a tip here in the studio for a horse called Colonel Collins. Now I don't know a lot about horseracing – but I believe he won the race last year

> Comment from a Jersey radio station, previewing the Derby, reported by SIMON HOLT *Sporting Life* 6 June 1994

If I was given a choice I wouldn't like to pick out the one I'd want to ride if I wasn't on Khamaseen.

> Er, yes, LESTER, that's as clear as mud! The maestro had been asked by Tim Richards which horse he'd like to be on if he wasn't riding Khamaseen in the Derby *Racing Post* 1 June 1994

He's not very big but he's got a motor.

> Well, that would certainly have helped Jermyn Street to win at Sandown for TOTE CHERRY-DOWNES *Racing Post* 1 June 1994

This horse talks to me and tells me when he's right.

> And trainer COLIN WILLIAMS is still allowed to walk around the streets despite claiming that he converses with his Worcester winner Our Slimbridge *Racing Post* 1 June 1994

It's like a severe kick in the balls.

> GEORGE DUFFIELD on being replaced on 2000 Guineas contender Unblest *Racing Post* 30 April 1994

The unpronounceable Irkutsk is 14/1.

> Commentator on SIS, having just pronounced the offending name, 14 April 1994

There's no money in writing books about racing. Half the racing world can't read and the other half is skint.

> And so say all of us! Comment attributed to the late ROGER MORTIMER who died in 1991 aged 82 and who wrote the classic *The History of the Derby Stakes* published in 1961

Peter O'Sullevan is the race of voicing.

> Attributed to RICHARD PITMAN by the *Racing Post* December 1993

And what about Opera House, will he go on the bog?

> Channel 4's DEREK THOMPSON previewing the Arc de Triomphe *Racing Post* December 1993

The House should know I have never eaten, and will never eat, a horse.

> NICHOLAS SOAMES, Minister for Food, with a message to Parliament which the thoroughbred population of the land will have been relieved to hear *Sporting Life* 26 March 1994

His secret

He [John Tuck] admitted his secret was using goose-grease on the gelding's legs.

> *Racing Post* report on trainer John Tuck's feat on winning a race with former cripple Connemara Dawn at Newton Abbot on 3 May 1994. If it has that effect on a broken-down horse, what could goose-grease do for you and me?

Nobody can deny that the emotive word 'winner' is an ardent description of a horse that has completed its task in the fastest time.

> No, no one can deny it, but I can't think of anyone else who would want to *say* it! Racing writer DAVEY TOWEY reported by Monty Court in the *Sporting Life* 13 May 1994

Foyer blew up, having suffered a hiccup in March.

> But the MICHAEL STOUTE-trained runner still managed to win at York in May! *Sporting Life* 13 May 1994

The bizarre thought of Willie Carson looking like Britt Ekland came from two separate quarters this week.

> The *Daily Mail*'s ALAN FRASER commenting on entries for a look-alike competition *Daily Mail* 26 March 1994

Did you see me on the radio?

> Excited jockey TONY DOBBIN to his changing room valet after landing his first Cheltenham Festival victory on Dizzy in the County Hurdle *Daily Telegraph* 19 March 1994

Guy Harwood would not run unless he had a chance.

> From the Teletext Derby Preview of 31 May 1994. I yield to no man in my admiration for Guy Harwood, but surely even Seb Coe wouldn't have a chance in the Derby, let alone Guy.

They've got well under just over two circuits to go.

SIS commentary at Ayr, 20 January 1994

I can state categorically that by far the majority of non-triers are engineered by bookmakers.

TIM FITZGEORGE-PARKER *Raceform Update* 22 January 1994

Linney Head is a generous horse at home.

JOHN GOSDEN, suggesting, perhaps, that his leading three-year-old would offer to share his box with all and sundry or would gladly hand out his grub to fellow inmates *Sporting Life* 14 May 1994

No danger, this wins.

It didn't, and this advertising phrase earned *Racing Telegraph* tipping service a breach of conduct ruling from the Independent Committee for the Supervision of Telephone Information Services *Sporting Life* 4 February 1994

Baydon Star was such a gentleman you could take him up to bed with you.

DAVID NICHOLSON after the tragic loss following a fall of his Baydon Star *Sporting Express* 22 May 1994

Non-users see it as something other people do.

Earth-shatteringly insightful comment by Ladbroke Marketing Controller JOHN O'REILLY, quizzed by *Marketing Week* magazine on how betting shops are viewed by those who don't frequent them, 13 May 1994

Toffee pudding

The Sussex course resembled a sticky toffee pudding.

A sweet description of Goodwood by *Sporting Life*'s GEOFF LESTER *Sporting Life* 19 May 1994

It was unbelievable – a massacre.

Not, as you may believe, a description of some mass killing by terrorists or bloodthirsty mercenaries – just one horse, Turtle Island, beating another, Grand Lodge, by 20 lengths in the Irish 2000 Guineas. The reaction of Grand Lodge's trainer WILLIAM JARVIS *Daily Mirror* 17 May 1994

He was a pure gentleman.

> Who could this mean? A respected old trainer? A veteran owner? No!
> Stud owner LIAM CASHMAN was speaking of recently deceased top jump
> stallion Strong Gale *Racing Post* 17 May 1994

We're still going for it and will continue to do so until we're past the lollipop.

> Richard Dunwoody's agent ROBERT PARSONS as his man moved seven
> winners ahead of title challenger Adrian Maguire with 11 days left
> *Racing Post* 23 May 1994

He was a bit disappointing last year when he was very top-heavy and had a wind problem.

> Yes, I know a few like that! Owner PETER SAVILL after his Harpoon Louie
> won at Ayr *Racing Post* 25 May 1994

He's just like a human sometimes. If, for some reason, we can't take him to Kingwood after racing he whinnies when the box drives by.

> Not like any human I know! Strange definition of the human race,
> courtesy of trainer JOHN HILLS, discussing his horse Gilderdale, as
> reported by Mark Popham *Weekender* 28 May 1994

You'll see a different horse at Epsom.

> HENRY CECIL, apparently revealing a 'ringer' plot for the Derby while
> referring to his King's Theatre, who had disappointed in the 2000
> Guineas and Dante *Daily Express* 26 May 1994. One wonders which
> 'different' horse he had in mind – the previous year's winner
> Commander In Chief, perhaps!

Willie Carson had his jacket off from halfway when Subya became outpaced.

> A topless Willie Carson, according to JAMES LAMBIE in the *Sporting Life* –
> that I would like to have seen! *Sporting Life* 28 May 1994

No matter what anyone says this is an honest Christian of a horse.

> Trainer HENRY BELL confirming the religious tendencies of his Cartmel
> winner Hellcatmudwrestler, whose name would seem to suggest
> otherwise! *Racing Post* 30 May 1994

THE GRAND NATIONAL

Bound to happen

It was bound to happen one day and it just happened that I had to be in charge at the time.

> Captain Keith Brown, Starter of the 1993 'Non' National *Weekender* 8 January 1994

Captain Keith Brown still blames everybody else. Racecourse management, impatient jockeys, screaming spectators, a needlessly long parade. And the protestors' smoke bombs. Starter Brown may be right in every detail. But won't you be relieved not to see him on the rostrum?

> MIKE LANGLEY, on the run-up to the 1994 race *Daily Mirror* 28 March 1994

Knicker elastic.

> JENNY PITMAN's dismissive description of the starting tape

It was bound to happen one day

If they get on to the course, let the horses gallop over them. That'll stop them.

> Red Rum's trainer GINGER McCAIN'S uncompromising solution to the problem of animal rights protestors at the Grand National *Up Front* Granada TV, March 1994

In sporting terms it was a cock-up and that is how I described it. Nobody got killed, no horse died and no jockey died. It was simply a sporting cock-up.

> DESMOND LYNAM on the 1993 National *Sporting Life* 9 April 1994

It was a very unfortunate incident. I feel very sorry for the people involved and for the millions who had a stake in the race.

> JOHN MAJOR

It was horrible. I died out there like the rest of us. It was a nightmare, a disaster.

> Starter KEITH BROWN on TV

It wasn't a disaster. Two young boys getting killed in Warrington was a disaster.

> Trainer CHARLIE BROOKS

Take a trip to Bosnia, the Sudan or even your local hospital. The Grand National being declared void isn't the end of the world. In fact, it is not really very important at all, is it?

> G. HAMMOND of Sandhurst, Surrey, letter to *Racing Post*

The Aintree executive wouldn't even give me the [winner's] rug for the horse, so I had one specially made for him.

> JENNY PITMAN *Racing Post* 24 January 1994

This race is not actually taking place.

> Aintree racecourse commentator during 1993 shambles

You must stop this race. My bloody horse has already gone one circuit. I don't want to win the National like this.

> Irate JENNY PITMAN during the 'race'

I thought the others had fallen or something.

> Esha Ness jockey JOHN WHITE. 'Or something' was about right.

Starter cocked it up . . . Aintree cocked it up . . . Jockey Club cocked it up.

> Only slight over-statement from *The Sun*

I wouldn't rob you of your money, love.

> Bookie RICHARD HALLING turning down prescient punter Judy Higby who tried to place a bet in his Tring betting shop that the National wouldn't take place, on the very morning of the event

I don't mind talking to the press, but finding your home surrounded 24 hours a day was hard.

> Starter KEITH BROWN *Daily Mail*

To restage the race outside its traditional time-slot would devalue it.

> Jockey Club statement explaining refusal to run the National later in the year

We had very strong advice from our own lawyers to do it, but what's the point?

> William Hill MD JOHN BROWN explaining the company's decision not to sue for expenses incurred as a result of the void National

The biggest loser

The biggest loser will be the Treasury.

Financial Times

At least no one will have backed a loser this year.

GRAHAM SHARPE of William Hill

A fiasco waiting to happen.

RICHARD EVANS, racing correspondent of *The Times*

I'd be strung up by the nuts.

Melbourne Cup Starter PAUL AHERN, asked what would happen to him if he emulated the National fiasco

It wouldn't be too difficult to have a flashing light saying 'Jockeys stop'; most jockeys can read.

Suggestion from former jockey BILL SMITH

So much for the luck of the Irish.

Journalist ALAN RUDDOCK whose correctly predicted Tricast bet, forecasting first, second and third in the 1993 National, would have won him £3000. Instead he got his money back.

National '94

I can't get the race out of my system. Possibly it is because I never won it. Perhaps those who have won it have their appetite sated. But after Crisp and now that Mark [his jockey son] has retired, I suppose the only way I'm going to be a winner is to own the bloody thing. I breed horses just with that in mind.

RICHARD PITMAN *Racing Post* 9 April 1994

It may sound strange, but when you ride out on the course, you really do feel the spirits of all the horses who've won it in the past.

PETER SCUDAMORE on riding in the Grand National *Radio Times* 26 March-1 April 1994

Any fatalities will immediately be laid at our door in triumph by those who profess to love animals, yet still relish the odd corpse to give grist to their mill.

Pre-race comment by ALASTAIR DOWN *Sporting Life* 1994

I don't believe the rubbish written about the start, that it's not important. Every inch of ground gained will be a help towards the end of the race. Short heads win races.

PETER SCUDAMORE on the National, which he never won *Daily Mail* 9 April 1994

Ten years ago I would not have run a horse in the Grand National because the race was killing horses.

Trainer JOHN UPSON, November 1993

We have been notified there may be plans to stage a demonstration using aircraft, parachutists, hang-gliders or even microlights. If people are prepared to use such irrational means, there is little we could do to stop them.

What turned out, fortunately, to be a somewhat over the top warning of imminent Battle of Britain-style Aintree invasion by animal rights protestors, delivered by INSPECTOR RAY SIMPSON of Merseyside Police on the eve of the 1994 National *Daily Telegraph* 9 April 1994

What better way could there be for them to sabotage the race than have a remote control which operates the starting gate before everyone is ready.

> JOHN SEXTON in the *Sporting Life* on possible animal rights tactics for the 1994 National

One person suggested the first fence should be on a hydraulic runner which could be raised to 20 feet in the event of a false start.

> Aintree MD CHARLES BARNETT

Press that button, pal, whatever happens.

> JENNY PITMAN's message on BBC TV to new Starter, Simon Morant

Pain and death, you bet. Please stay away on Grand National Day.

> Poster flourished by animal rights protestors at Aintree

We are no longer animal-loving eccentrics who go too far. We are now a well-trained secret army. Every time a horse dies in the National we will step up our campaign.

> Animal rights activist ROY PATTERSON *Sporting Life* 6 March 1994

It was on New Year's Day 1983. I used to live near Windsor and I went racing for the day, and ended up backing a horse called Seymour's Lady. She won the seller by 25 lengths and I bought it in the auction for 2000 Guineas. That was the start of things.

> How FREDDIE STARR set off on the road to owning Grand National winner Miinnehoma *Racing Post* 11 April 1994

Winning the race was better than marriage and even better than sex. I had placed a total of £10,000 on the horse through lots of scattered bets put on by friends. If I had walked into a bookie and put on that amount of money, it would have been on a hotline all over the country.

> FREDDIE STARR, after Miinnehoma's victory, showing considerable knowledge of the way bookies work, but casting doubt on his own sexual experiences!

McCain is a homophobic, misogynist bastard.

> KENNETH CONDON of Canterbury in a letter to *The Observer* 10 April 1994 after trainer Ginger McCain had declared that he didn't want the National becoming 'a race for poofters and girls', while J.C. Durkin of Southport took Ginger further to task as (s)he pointed out that the race had been 'the exclusive preserve of poofters and girls – referred to as geldings and mares in polite circles – from the year dot'.

Officers seized incendiary devices, German-made flares, and hand-cuffs which they believe were to be used by protestors to lock themselves to fences. Five metal detectors were used to avert a potential threat that spikes could be scattered on the course.

> *Sunday Post* 10 April 1994

Bloody good.

> How Starter SIMON MORANT was feeling after getting the runners away successfully *Racing Post* 11 April 1994

Hey, what the hell are you doing here?

> RICHARD DUNWOODY at Becher's, second time round, shocked to see Simon Burrough on Just So, once nicknamed Just Slow, on level terms *The Times* 11 April 1994

If the Grand National was cruel, we would have no right to enjoy it. If it is not cruel, we need to let the public hear us say so with confidence and without defensiveness.

> ROBIN COOK, Shadow Spokesman on Trade and Industry *Sporting Life* 11 April 1994

Always be confident

Always be confident. Hack around the first circuit, towards the outside to avoid trouble, then crack on second time.

> Good advice from three times winning jockey BRIAN FLETCHER *The Independent* 5 April 1994

Not to put it too bluntly, it seemed to me that some of them thought I should be tied to a gunwheel and flogged for being an insubordinate little prick.

> BERNARD DONIGAN, equine consultant to the RSPCA, on his first meeting with the Jockey Club to consider safety modifications to the National fences *The Observer* 3 April 1994

I don't think it's a race for women riders, although I expect that eventually a horse will be good enough to carry one round as a passenger to win.

> Trainer GINGER McCAIN *The Observer* 3 April 1994

I've seen that description in countless newspaper headlines and it's not true. I've no children.

> ROSEMARY 'The Galloping Granny' HENDERSON *Daily Record* 15 April 1994

Thank God I've got here. I'm not too late for the National, am I?

> He wasn't too late but, sadly for this racegoer, he'd turned up at Haydock Park instead of Aintree. Still, he was able to watch the Manchester Dog Show instead! *Racing Post* 15 April 1994

had backed Moorcroft Boy.

> Apparent case of disloyalty from CAROL DUNWOODY (wife of Richard, who rode the winner), who went on to explain: 'Of course I wanted Richard to win but it would have been the kiss of death if I backed him' *Daily Mirror* 15 April 1994

To more serious matters – the Grand National, which according to John Dixon, from Hawkhurst, Kent, is not so grand at all.

'Do racing commentators wear blinkers?' asks Mr Dixon. 'After reading your Grand National coverage, the answer must be yes. 'Regained its pride' wrote Graham Rock. 'A classic' wrote Paul Wilson, echoing the hyperbole of Des Lynam and co. Perhaps they can explain the glory of a race in which 82 per cent of the runners failed to finish, where some had odds of 200/1 and where, as Barry Hugill bravely reported on your news pages, 'The loudest cheers seemed to come every time a horse fell.'

'Exceptionally', said the BBC, 'there were no serious injuries', implying that these were the norm, an acceptable part of the day's entertainment. I could have switched off and avoided the gruesome spectacle of animals crashing into fences and each other. But then would I have been able to protest at the barbarity of the event and its scandalous coverage if I had? Shame on all of you.

> Letter to *The Observer* 17 April 1994, from a man who is never likely to be invited to join the Jockey Club but who at least makes his argument in a reasoned and rational manner

[Freddie] Starr claims to have taken £330,000 off bookmakers by telling 20 friends to fan out across the country with £10,000 in stake money. He should have had a word with 76-year-old Louisa Day who backed the first four home but wins only £3.87. Her bets range from a daring 5p each way to a positively reckless 10p.

> PAUL HAYWARD *Daily Telegraph* 16 April 1994

The starting procedures for tomorrow's Grand National have been modernised, we are told. There will be no repeat of last year's spectacular fiasco. What a shame. For many, the glorious cock-up was the only interesting thing about it. A normal race is all very well for the racing buffs, but for connoisseurs of the Great British Disaster it is a bit of a disappointment.

> Leader column comment in London's *Evening Standard* on the eve of the race

Bookies 'Ate Freddie Starr

> *The Sun*'s headline after Miinnehoma's owner claimed betting winnings of some £300,000, which recalled the epic Freddie Starr Ate My Hamster headline of some years earlier

CONTRARY VIEWS

Will they race at Ascot?

Chances practically nil.

SIR NICKY BEAUMONT, 12 January 1994

The situation has improved no end. If the forecast proves accurate acing should take place.

Ascot, 13 January 1994

2/5 to race at Ascot.

Bookies Victor Chandler, 13 January 1994

Racing abandoned.

Ascot, 14 January 1994

It is silly

get fed up hearing complaints about the tracks out here. It is silly. They are fair with wonderfully designed bends.

French trainer ANDRE FABRE on the Santa Anita course just hours before his Arcangues landed a 133/1 shock on the Breeders Cup Classic *Sporting Life* November 1993

It's a lousy course – period!

British trainer in the USA, MICHAEL DICKINSON, on the Santa Anita racecourse used for the Breeders' Cup Series *Today* November 1993

One owner recently sent 14 horses to a trainer based at Santa Anita nd they all broke down within weeks.

MICHAEL DICKINSON *Today* November 1993

Don't panic. Talk amongst yourselves.

> DEREK THOMPSON, hosting a closed-circuit screening from the USA of the
> 1992 Breeders' Cup, to diners at London's Savoy Hotel, reacting to Lester
> Piggott's crashing fall, as reported by Peter Hilton *Racing Post* 29 March
> 1993

This was not quite how Mr Thompson remembered the occasion, as
he explained. 'I tried to calm the situation by advising people not to
panic and to keep things going on as normal. May I suggest that Mr
Hilton might have had a little too much liquid refreshment that
evening as, apart from misquoting my speech, he seems to have
forgotten the venue – we were at the Café Royal.'

> *Racing Post* 30 March 1993

A complete rip-off.

> JULIAN WILSON's view of premium-rated telephone tipping lines, in
> December 1993

To assume everybody who runs a raceline is out to con people
shows gross naivety.

> Letter to *Sporting Life* 9 December 1993, from MARK HOLDER of Bristol

To show it potentially being killed was poor judgement.

> National Trainers' Federation President PETER CUNDELL

We were prepared at all times to switch the picture away from the
horse if it looked as though he was going to do himself serious dam
age.

> Channel 4 spokesman. Contrasting opinions as to whether C4 were
> right to show pictures of a blindfolded horse which had escaped the
> stalls handlers running free around Doncaster racecourse. *Sporting Life*
> 30 March 1993

If it were Japanese, Czechoslovakian, Arabic, Chinese or French
they would have it perfect. But if it is Irish you will have the great
est bastardisation of all times.

> Extraordinary comment by a member of the Dublin Parliament, AUSTIN
> DEASY, who was accusing British racing commentators of 'deliberately
> insulting the Irish people' by mispronouncing the names of horses from
> the Republic *Daily Telegraph* 30 April 1994

Sometimes, where an Irish horse is concerned you can ring up half a dozen of its connections and they'll all pronounce it differently themselves.

> PETER O'SULLEVAN, himself half-Irish, countering criticism of commentators' pronunciation of Irish horses' names *Daily Mail* 7 May 1994

I regard Mr Austin Deasy as the prat of yet another week in which no progress was made towards stopping the murder just up the road from his debating chamber.

> IAN WOOLDRIDGE putting the row over racehorse name pronunciation into perspective *Daily Mail* 7 May 1994

I don't like seeing a game horse hit, but after all this was the Derby.

> SIR JACK JARVIS, trainer of Pretendre, beaten a neck by Charlottown in 1966 when his jockey Paul Cook didn't use his whip and rival Scobie Breasly did *History of the Derby Stakes* Roger Mortimer, Michael Joseph, 1973

Beating animals in the name of sport is unacceptable.

> JOHN McCRIRICK on ITV's *Sport in Question* 23 May 1994

On a par

I have been to 22 racecourses in Great Britain and only Sandown and Ascot are even on a par with a typical American track in terms of facilities, if by facilities are meant sufficient viewing areas with seats, large and comfortable indoor spaces with an ample number of bars, snack bars, cafeterias and souvenir stands, and outdoor picnic areas.

> *Sporting Life's* US correspondent ALAN SHUBACK, 20 May 1994

The best racecourses in Britain offer facilities and entertainment far superior to anything available to racegoers anywhere in Europe or North America.

> JOCELYN DE MOUBRAY *Pacemaker & Thoroughbred Breeder* May 1994. Ah well, yer pays yer money.

The conflicting reports concerning the need, or not, for 'cut in the ground' led me to believe that Turtle Island is simply not likely to run up to classic-winning ability on any ground.

I bet Turtle Island will not win a classic, and probably he will not win a Group One race over a mile either this year – on any ground. I will lay £300–£250 against the former, provided that if I have to pay up, the proceeds go to charity.

> MICHAEL HARVEY, Edgbaston, Birmingham, in a letter to *Sporting Life* 5 May 1994 after Turtle Island failed to run in the 2000 Guineas

In the wake of Sunday's triumphant win at the Curragh I owe Peter Chapple-Hyam an apology.

> MICHAEL HARVEY, Edgbaston, Birmingham, after Turtle Island won the Irish 2000 Guineas in runaway style. Letter to *Sporting Life* 20 May 1994

I was sad to read that the 1994 Derby will be the last to bear the prefix Ever Ready.

> HENRY CECIL

Eleven years the Derby has languished under Ever Ready's sponsorship. During this time the race has lost both quality and prestige.

> Racing writer PAUL HAIGH

Because of Mr Dettori's caution for being in possession of drugs he will not be allowed to ride in Japan.

> DR OSAMU SUGIMOTO, Manager of Japan Racing Association's London office

I have not applied for a licence to ride in Japan and accordingly have not been denied a licence.

> FRANKIE DETTORI, in late 1993

I told him he could not start white mice.

> Slightly miffed DAVID NICHOLSON to Starter Simon Morant at Aintree in November 1993 after his Meleagris failed to start

I don't think the horse would have started if I'd waited until tomorrow.

> SIMON MORANT

GAMBLING

Lost her shirt

This week Ladbroke will bombard the punters with a new advertising campaign for its betting shops. Plastered across a picture of racing gee-gees will be the slogan: Don't forget, Lady Godiva put everything she had on a horse. It's snappy, cheeky, eye-catching even, and Ladbroke probably paid the advertising agency handsomely. But there is one niggle: what on earth does it mean? The connection with betting that springs to my mind is that Lady Godiva completely lost her shirt.

> Business writer RICHARD WOODS *Sunday Times* 15 April 1994

There is no doubt that there are people listening in to calls into and from racecourses.

> Racecourse bookie ANDREW PETER alleging that scanning equipment is being used to eavesdrop on mobile phone calls at the races – with dishonest intent *Racing Post* 4 February 1994

I'm a greedy man doing it for the money.

> Owner of The Illiad, NOEL FURLONG, who laid 'my biggest ever single gamble' of some £200,000 on his horse to win him £3m in the Ladbroke Hurdle. It was unplaced *Daily Express* 10 January 1994

People rarely believe us, but we can't afford to bet.

> Trainer ROGER SPICER after his 440/1 double with two 20/1 winners at Southwell on 8 November 1993 *Sporting Life* 7 January 1994

We did no good on Saturday but we'll get it back today.

> Refreshing honesty in *Sporting Life* advert for tipster 'The Springbok', 11 January 1994

£&'/\'d3$.!\'d3

> Believed to be the comments of the punter who stepped in to take advantage of the tempting 1/16 chalked up about Suluk at Southwell in February 1993. He risked £3,200. It lost, returning 1/14. He didn't even get the value!

She had a big chance but there was no way I could back her. After the way Winter Belle got stuffed at Cheltenham I swore I'd never seriously fancy one of mine again.

> Irish trainer PADDY PRENDERGAST on why he didn't back Irish Lincolnshire winner Soundproof, following the defeat of supposed 'good thing' Winter Belle *Racing Post* 13 April 1994

He wasn't English and is dead now but I won't even tell you the horse because it would lead you to the name of the man and I won't identify any of my clients.

> Bookie VICTOR CHANDLER on the man who lost £250,000 on a 2/5 shot *Racing Post* 15 January 1994

To buy a thrill.

> *Channel 4 Racing* executive producer ANDREW FRANKLIN, asked 'Why do you bet?' *Weekender* 8 January 1994

Most punters do not give a monkey's if Adrian Maguire slaps, kisses or does an Irish jig with his mount provided he gets it over the line first when their money is on him.

> Letter-writer F. DAVIES of Sheffield *Racing Post* 25 January 1994

When I started training I thought betting was a way to easy money. It didn't take me long to learn it wasn't and, with one exception when it went badly wrong, I haven't had a bet for 12 years.

Irish trainer MICHAEL HOURIGAN *Racing Post* 3 February 1994

Only tip

The only tip I can give on jumpers is – where to buy them in London!

Flat trainer HENRY CECIL *Racing Post* November 1993

It's an established fact: the one with the biggest nostrils always wins.

Anonymous Aussie racegoer at the Melbourne Cup 1993, reported by ROBERT PHILIP of the *Daily Telegraph*, who didn't ask whether the punter was referring to horses or jockeys!

I do not back odds-on favourites. You can buy money at the bank – you don't have to buy it at Ladbrokes.

Irish Premier ALBERT REYNOLDS *Sporting Life* 10 January 1994

Cogent is a nice enough horse, but will find this too far and most of these too good.

PAUL HAIGH at the *Racing Post* on 1993 10/1 Hennessy winner Cogent

I gotta horse!

Rallying cry of racecourse tipster PRINCE MONOLULU who died in 1965 aged 84 but for many years appeared at all the major meetings dispensing advice for a small fee in a flamboyant style matched only by his exotic garb, pre-dating by a few decades our modern-day equivalent, John 'Big Mac' McCririck

I would not advise people to back him.

Trainer MARTIN PIPE, on the chances of Miinnehoma making a successful comeback at Newbury after a 399-day absence. The horse won at 11/2, 5 March 1994

Skin 'em and burn' em

We're gonna skin 'em and burn 'em, the punters, today.

> Bookie BARRY DENNIS featured at Newmarket in a December 1993 Anglia
> TV documentary *The Big Day* just prior to doing his dough!

When I came into racing and bookmaking it was the Sport of Kings;
now it is the den of rats. So many people have forgotten how to act
honourably.

> 54-year-old Irish bookmaker BILLY ARKLE. *BOS* magazine, November 1993

The bookmakers again showed they can give MI6 a good run for
their money in gathering information,

> RICHARD EDMONDSON on the fact that bookies knew that Fortune And
> Fame, the Champion Hurdle favourite, would miss the race before any
> official word was forthcoming *The Independent* 14 March 1994

I've had more memorable days.

> Irish mega-punter/bookie J.P. McMANUS, who had allegedly lost £200,000
> at the first day of the Cheltenham Festival *Daily Express* 18 March 1994

He is without doubt the biggest gambler in Britain.

> BBC's GRAHAM ROCK on J.P. McManus *Daily Express* 18 March 1994

We'll leave the Pope out of our next advertising campaign. Anyway,
we stand to lose half a million pounds if he does sign for Rangers
and plays only one game.

> STEWART KENNY, MD of Irish bookies Paddy Power, censured by the
> Advertising Standards Authority for running an ad campaign offering
> odds of 100,000/1 against the Pope signing for Glasgow Rangers *Daily
> Star* 16 March 1994

I don't bet.

> Trainer JOHN MANNERS, revealing he'd had £1 each way on his 100/1
> Leicester winner Killeshin *Racing Post* 9 March 1994

It must be a good idea – it was invented by me.

> LORD WYATT on the Tote's QuadPot bet *Sporting Life* 9 March 1994

He is now 42, and says that if I'd started with £500 on December 3 and backed every horse he told me to, I would have £86,000 now. 'Really?' I said. 'Do you have £86,000 now?' He explained that unfortunately he didn't, because he'd broken his own first rule of gambling and switched from geometrical to arithmetical progression. 'What does that mean?' I asked. 'It means I spent it.'

> LYNN BARBER on 'professional gambler' Richard McLaughlin *Sunday Times* 20 March 1994

We want it to be more like dealing with your stockbroker than with your brothel keeper.

> LINDSAY McNEILE, director of spread betting company Sporting Index. What *can* he mean? *Sporting Life* 4 February 1994

Lottery

The lottery is the biggest threat that has ever approached racing and betting shops.

> Owner of 40 betting shops PETER SMITH *Sporting Life* 4 January 1994

With his Cheshire Cat grin, Baker always looked as if he could have a secret sideline as a sleek-haired bookie. (Risk a fiver with Honest Ken!)

> PAUL BARKER of *The Times* with one of the most insulting remarks about bookies I've ever come across, comparing them to the then Tory Home Secretary who proposed the National Lottery in a 1992 White Paper *The Times* 26 May 1994

I don't anticipate betting turnover will be deeply affected. Of course, there will be some effect but the lottery is a different ball game to going into a betting shop.

> Chief Executive of National Lottery organisers Camelot, TIM HOLLEY *Sporting Life* 26 May 1994

We will bridge a gap of more than 126 years since the last lottery. It will become woven into the national fabric, like the Grand National, Derby and Cup Final, except the National Lottery is every week.

> DAVID RIGG, Communications Director of National Lottery organisers Camelot *Sporting Life* 25 May 1994

People should not be encouraged to gamble and bookies are a bit like a toilet, you know where it is and you go and use it when you want to.

> The enlightened and ungrammatical views of the tolerant CHRIS FAIRBAIRN who, incredibly enough, was speaking as Jersey's Gambling Control Officer when quoted by the island's paper, the *Jersey Post*, in August 1993

Yours faithfully

Wed 11th April 1990

Dear Sirs,

I won four hundred and seventy five pounds in a bet with your company four years ago, involving two horses, but I now do not want the money and I am therefore returning it to you, to do what you think/feel is best, ie put it back into horse racing or into a charity of your choice. An extra twenty five pounds has been added for the trouble to which this letter/money puts you ie book-keeping and money transfer.

Total enclosed is five hundred pounds in Postal Orders.

Yours faithfully,

Mr M

> An almost unbelievable letter received by William Hill in 1990 – they donated the money to a racing charity

8 October 1988

Dear Sir,

On Friday 07 October 1988, I placed a wager in your Eastcheap Office. Despite the normally overwhelming burden of carrying my money and my confidence, by some unprecedented miracle, the horse still managed to pass the post in first place. I anxiously awaited for the Stewards Enquiry to be announced so that my sole winner of the season could then subsequently be disqualified and I could yet again talk about the 'one that got away'. The Stewards seemed strangely unaware that I had actually backed a winner and the only announcement forthcoming was 'They've weighed in'.

Having taken my special tablets to control my heart palpitation and waited for general euphoria to subside, the time was ripe to present that rarest of documents – the *winning slip* !!! Alas it had gone astray since I could not control that unbreakable habit of discarding all slips on the grounds that all slips are losing slips. Not to worry, I thought, simply present a copy of the bet and I will be paid. It was not to be !!! Because of the 'vast fortune' involved I was informed that I would have to write to you – hence this letter.

Both the Counter Clerk, who accepted the wager, and the Manager of the shop remember me distinctly, since I not only have a passing resemblance to Robert Redford, on a bad day, in poor light, but because they had to contact Head Office before laying the bet. Perhaps I also have a passing resemblance to Barney Curley and they were instilled with fear of a monster payout.

I enclose a copy of the remarkable wager and trust you will give this matter your most urgent consideration so that I will have funds to indulge my favourite pastime of backing certainties that have an uncanny, incredible, almost unbelievable knack of finishing second. I will of course provide documentary evidence of my true identity and address.

Yours faithfully

> A letter received by William Hill Customer Relations Manager Steve Frater, who arranged for the customer to be paid

Punter

Hostesses equipped with PenPad will roam through the restaurants and around the grandstand at the track, accepting bets as they go. The punter asks the odds, the PenPad receives the data from the main computer and displays it. The hostess accepts the bet, a portable printer produces a betting slip and the transaction is radioed back to the main computer.

> *Sunday Times* report on the potential for a 'Mobile Bookie' using a Toshiba PenPad, 10 April 1994

Don't worry, Tommo – what you don't have you don't miss.

> Words of cold comfort from JOHN FRANCOME to Derek Thompson after the latter had five winners and a runner-up beaten into second in a photo in his Jackpot bet which would have won him £100,000 *Sporting Life* 16 April 1994

I speak with the dubious authority of one who . . . stopped or anyway steered a long way round on a possible winner because, not realising how badly she needed fast ground, we had not a penny on her and I could not afford the training fees without a bet.

> Confession of LORD OAKSEY, revealing that he was fined just £25 and that the horse, Cautious, won next time out at 6/1 *Daily Telegraph* 24 January 1994

They show no odds but merely lean across to their prospective client with the air of a priest in a confessional and listen to the sins he would like to commit.

> MICK CLEARY on rails bookies at Cheltenham *The Observer* 20 March 1994

Apparently there have been a few cases where this had happened. Unfortunately, even if the cardholder wins he can't keep the money because it is a mistaken transaction. Equally, if the fraudster uses the card to place a bet and loses, we will refund the stake to the cardholder.

> TIM GREEN, General Manager of Switch, the debit card system on which stolen cards have been used by the thieves to place bets – not realising that any winnings will be credited to the person in whose name the card is registered *Sunday Times* 17 April 1994

I have about eight bets a year on my own horses. My biggest ever bet was £500. I don't really get a lot of pleasure from it, whereas father absolutely loves it. He's always liked to have a punt; it's a challenge to him.

> Trainer JOHN HILLS, whose Dad Barry has long been acknowledged as a threat to the Ring *Sunday Times* 15 April 1994

For many Christians, horseracing is a no-go area because of the gambling. This has always seemed very selective to me. The same people who tut-tut at the High Street betting shop, and ignore the Ladbrokes stand at Test matches, perhaps fill their pools coupon and ring their stockbrokers regularly. Horseracing is only quantitatively more dependent on gambling than other sports. There is no difference in principle.

> THE REVEREND ANDREW WINGFIELD DIGBY, director of Christians in Sport *The Observer* 15 May 1994

We do not remember a Jackpot meeting being called off after one race, and it's doubtful that there's been a smaller dividend.

> Tote spokesman GEOFFREY WEBSTER after Brighton's meeting was abandoned after one race following heavy rain with the result that a Tote jackpot dividend of just 15.6–1 was paid *Racing Post* 27 May 1994

We had him at 10,000/1 to be the next Pope. I suppose we will have to adjust the odds now.

> Irish bookie PAT BAMBURY on his cousin Father Donal Bambury who launched Doncaster's trial Sunday meeting with a service, and was promoted to Monsignor *Racing Post* 27 May 1994

The phrase you are least likely to hear in a betting shop after a race is 'I was wrong'.

> From a *Sunday Times* article of 29 May 1994

Maybe she wanted some tips for the last 10 days of the jumps season.

> CHESTER BARNES on a lunch organised by the Queen Mother to which his boss, Martin Pipe, and a number of other racing figures were invited *Sporting Life* 25 May 1994

I'm not opposed to having a bet, and if I can't make money out of the game, who can? I could be sitting in a horsebox for eight hours so I get plenty of time to study. Punters who pick up a newspaper for five minutes before having a bet don't deserve to make money.

> ROBERT HAMILTON, travelling head lad to John Dunlop *Sporting Life* 20 May 1994

Generally it is an 'odds-to' basis. But if they are from a big yard and they come on every day and say 'that's fancied, that's not, that is' then it is more of a wages type thing and you put them on the pay-roll and employ them as a member of staff.

> Fascinating insight by owner and tipping-line operator DARREN CROFT on how he rewards his 'contacts' for their information *Weekender* 19 February 1994

I've been gambling since the age of four, whether it was a game of cards or anything to make a bit of extra money on the side. Even as a stable lad I was betting three times more than I was earning. I would say that I've never not been winning. The bookies owe me nothing. I've certainly had a good life out of it.

> Trainer JOHN WHITE *Sunday Times* October 1993

You've got to think it was a great bit of entertainment for a quid.

> Sentiments with which punter Jason Mosley may not agree, having found 10 consecutive winners in his accumulator, only for the 11th to let him down for winnings of £43,000, producing these sensitive words of comfort from a Ladbroke spokesperson *Daily Telegraph* 2 April 1994

A wager on it

Imagine it's the Grand National and someone has put a wager on it and there's a Stewards Inquiry. They could easily misjudge the time.

> Airlines spokesman ROBERT SCHUMACHER, worrying about a betting shop set to open at Gatwick Airport *The Observer* 20 January 1994

I certainly don't make a profit but if you go racing there doesn't seem to be any point if you don't bet. I like an antepost bet as well and just like anyone else I back non runners. I'd backed Turtle Island for the 2000 Guineas. As you know he didn't run because of the ground. Bit of a mug-punter really.

> Mmm, maybe – not a mug owner or breeder, though! ROBERT SANGSTER revealing some of his betting habits to *The Guardian* 1 June 1994

Take it.

> WILLIE CARSON, on hearing that Derby hope Erhaab, on whom he had just won the Dante at York, was quoted at 5/1 for the Derby, BBC Radio 5, 12 May 1994

I'll collect over a million pounds if Mr Snugfit wins the big one tomorrow.

> Mega punter TERRY RAMSDEN on the eve of the 1986 Grand National. Mr Snugfit finished fourth, rewarding his owner's place wagers.

By mistake I handed the bookie 50 quid instead of 20. When I went to collect he wanted to know who'd tipped the horse. 'The owner,' I said. 'Me.'

> REG WILKINS on backing Double Silk to win at 10/1 at Cheltenham in 1993

It would be much simpler for all concerned if 6/4 were described as 2.5 times stake.

> KELVIN STACEY, Marketing Director of Coral *Sporting Life* 24 December 1993

Part of the remedy is in the hands of the public. If the horses which they have backed are not properly ridden they should take action, either writing or telephoning if away from the course, or booing, catcalling as in France, even, sometimes, throwing form books as in Australia although perhaps that would frighten the horses!

> Inciting punters to riot! TIM FITZGEORGE-PARKER *Raceform Update* 16 April 1994

Not so the fellow who watched the desperately close finish to Chester's opening race, the Lily Agnes Stakes, and was so convinced that Jack Berry's Tino Tere had got the verdict over Chandleigh House that he raced around the betting ring taking the odds on the outcome of the photo finish – an absolute certainty. He staked £2000 to win £100 and £1000 to win £50 (both 20/1 on) then £100 to win £100 (10/1 on) and a few smaller bets. Within a couple of minutes he had to face the awful truth that he was wrong! Chandleigh House was the winner by a short head.

> A cautionary tale from the *Daily Telegraph Flat Racing Yearbook* 1992 (Headline)

Today has been embarrassing – we took virtually no money for her at all.

> DON PAYNE of William Hill, barely disguising his glee at the victory of 50/1 outsider of nine Jet Ski Lady in the Oaks, 8 June 1991

It was my husband Bill who had the bet, but we are married and there is no rule against your husband betting.

> ROSEMARY HENDERSON on the £50 bet on her completing the course in the Grand National on Fiddlers Pike, struck at odds of 8/1, which earned her a 'gentle' knuckle rapping when the Jockey Club reminded her of the rules forbidding amateur riders from betting *Racing Post* 28 April 1994

SUNDAY RACING

It is humbug

Members of Parliament have a better chance than usual . . . to make an improvement in the quality of their constituents' lives. In a free vote . . . they should decide to legalise Sunday racing and bring Britain into line with the rest of the racing world. The laws that inhibit Sunday racing are socially as well as temporally obsolete, and they share a whiff of the old English vices of humbug and class. The Sabbatarian argument against Sunday racing is concerned with keeping Sunday special and the immorality of gambling on the Sabbath. This had more force when other professional sport was banned on Sunday. But Test matches, the Wimbledon men's final, Open golf, and Grand Prix motor racing now take place on Sundays, and it is rumoured that gambling takes place on all these sports. It is difficult to see the difference in principle that allows casinos to open on Sunday, but keeps betting shops closed. Anybody with a credit account can bet on racing on a Sunday at Longchamp or Leopardstown. It is humbug to pretend that Sunday is kept special by letting them gamble, while cash customers are kept out of the betting shops. No other god-fearing nation bans Sunday racing . . .

The only plausible argument against Sunday racing is that seven-day racing all the year round would put an unfair strain on those who work in racing. But theirs is a leisure industry, and Sunday has become the day for mass leisure . . .

There is no valid reason why the Sport of Kings and the Queen should remain the one exception to Sunday opening. Racing is not the property of the leisured classes who can take any day off. It is a great leisure industry for the masses. And that implies opening on the day of the week when most people are at leisure . . .

> A robust *Times* leader column comment in favour of Sunday racing with betting, printed on the day Parliament voted to permit it, 10 May 1994 . It could well have swung the issue.

Sir, An impression has been created that everyone wants Sunday racing. That is not true. We are aware of opposition from many quarters.

> Letter to *The Times* jointly by trainers HENRY CECIL and MICHAEL HEATON-ELLIS, which appeared on the same page as the paper's leader column in favour of Sunday racing

Switching a poorly promoted event to a Sunday is not going to transform its appeal at a stroke.

> JOCELYN DE MOUBRAY *Pacemaker & Thoroughbred Breeder* June 1994

I'm opposed to it on religious, sociological and pragmatic grounds.

> JULIAN WILSON *Daily Telegraph* 11 May 1994

If there is a public demand for more Sunday racing, then racing must answer it with a full programme. There isn't just one cricket match on a Sunday, or one cinema, or one theme park. They have not imposed artificial restrictions. Neither should racing. Racing and betting have to go for the mass Sunday audience, and they should not be deflected by those fearful of brash assaults on the fabric of our society.

> *Sporting Life* comment 11 May 1994

The way forward for Sunday is to provide a real family day out. I believe the way forward for racing is to offer families that day out.

> Labour Shadow Minister for Trade and Industry, ROBIN COOK *Racing Post* 11 May 1994

I think it is an abomination and one of the worst-thought-out concepts ever produced in racing. It will probably cost the industry money.

> JULIAN WILSON *Racing Post* 11 May 1994

The shape of an industry has been altered at a stroke under the guise of sweeping away a few archaic rules.

> ALASDAIR BARRON, Keep Sunday Special *Racing Post* 11 May 1994

There will be a hell of a lot more work involved for everybody and we will need to have a closed day so that everybody can have a breather.

> Trainer LUCA CUMANI

Stop racing on Monday and by all means race on Sunday.

> Trainer MICHAEL BELL

I like my Sundays at home but if there are rides to be had then I'll take them – it's my job.

> Jockey KEVIN DARLEY *Racing Post* 11 May 1994

Hasn't got a cat in hell's chance for 25 years.

> LORD WYATT on the prospects of Sunday racing with off-course betting, 14 December 1993. What a tipster!

Contrary to popular belief

Contrary to popular belief, most owners do work for a living during the week, so Sunday is a major leisure day for them, when they could enjoy at least an emotional return on their investment.

> JOHN BIGGS, Director General of the Racehorse Owners' Association, supporting Sunday racing *Racing Post* 5 May 1994

Even those of us who believe that many more lives will be blighted than enhanced must grin and bear it.

> IAN CARNABY *Sporting Life* 12 May 1994

The Church of England in particular should realise that it has done more than most to drive people to find other ways in which to spend their Sundays, so I hope it will not complain too loudly.

> Political commentator SIMON HEFFER *Daily Mail* 12 May 1994

I'm just an old-fashioned boy and I still think that Sunday is a special day and should stay that way for those of us involved in the racing business.

> Channel 4's DEREK THOMPSON *Daily Mirror* 12 May 1994

I believe that by the end of the century there will be racing on 52 Sundays in the year.

> Channel 4's JOHN McCRIRICK *Daily Mirror* 12 May 1994

TAILENDERS

I must admit

I must admit I haven't seen the race on video.

RICHARD DUNWOODY, revealing that he hadn't bothered to watch the Cheltenham Gold Cup run on 17 March, for which he had been suspended *Daily Mail* 9 April 1994

Research recently carried out by a national newspaper showed that 86 per cent of those surveyed had heard of Red Rum, but only 84 per cent claimed to have heard of the present Prime Minister, John Major.

Daily Mail 9 April 1994

There are two things in life guaranteed to get me excited. The first is Anna Lee tackled up in the stockings, the second is the start of the flat at Doncaster.

Tipster MARK WINSTANLEY *Sporting Life* 22 March 1994. Whatever turns you on!

This could be an excellent opportunity for a fast-food chain to introduce a new product for betting shop consumption, horseburgers.

What better to cheer a munching punter than the knowledge that the loser he backed three weeks ago did not turn out to be completely useless.

PETER CORRIGAN, discussing the widening range of snacks available to betting shop customers *Independent on Sunday* 13 March 1994

Michael O'Hehir, the former Irish commentator, was inadvertently referred to in yesterday's *Sporting Life* as the late Michael O'Hehir. We are happy to report that O'Hehir, now 73, is alive and kicking in his native Ireland.

Sporting Life 19 March 1994

Richard Pitman to Carol Dunwoody, discussing the latest addition to her photographic equipment, a splendidly long lens: 'I believe it's called Linford Christie.'

Carol Dunwoody: 'You're not supposed to know that.'

> BBC racing, 3 December 1993

I hope he has not hurt his foot.

> Veteran American trainer CHARLIE 'Bald Eagle' WHITTINGHAM after suffering a gashed head when his great champion Sunday Silence kicked him

Fast horses and beautiful women are the two things I love best.

> BALD EAGLE

We find it unbelievable that we have been banned from Epsom whose only claim to fame is horses.

> Circus man GERRY COTTLE on a council-imposed ban on the Cottle Circus playing at Epsom because it features horses

I was there at Cheltenham when Terry Biddlecombe announced his retirement from the saddle by hurdling the last fence in the near dark, without a horse, in the nude.

> TONY LEWIS *Daily Telegraph* 8 February 1994

Tool of Satan.

> Insult hurled at Houston Commission for Racing member Nathan Avery on TV when he dared to promote racing's cause in Texas where Grade 1 racing only resumed in April 1994 after a 57 year gap during most of which time Pari-mutuel wagering was illegal *Pacemaker & Thoroughbred Breeder* June 1994

I understand it is 13/8 against Egon Ronay publishing a Good Betting Shop Food Guide by 1997.

> CLEMENT FREUD *Sporting Life* 1 March 1994

Similar to bingo

We are sorting out how it will be done, but it is likely to be similar to bingo.

> Jockey Club medical adviser DR MICHAEL TURNER on the method of selecting which jockeys will be drug-tested *Sporting Life* 20 January 1994

This horse threatens to be better than either of those put together.

> I promise you I heard RICHARD PITMAN tell a TV audience that while discussing a runner's sire and dam

Can't really say, but whatever beats me will win it.

> JOHN FRANCOME replying when asked how his two-runner exhibition race against Lester Piggott was likely to go

He'll be useful if they give him a bit of time.

> Jockey JOE O'GORMAN on 13 March 1989 after 14-year-old jumper Panegyrist had won at Ayr – after 38 losing races

The racing fraternity consists very largely of a bunch of crooks out to relieve you of your money.

> MR JUSTICE MELFORD STEVENSON commenting during the course of a court case in January 1967

Meet back at the weighing room after we've caught him.

> Typically pessimistic instructions from trainer TIM FORSTER to connections of Last Suspect before that horse went out for the 1985 Grand National – which he won

John Higgins fractured a bone in his left leg in a fall from Mrs Higgins at Edinburgh on Monday, and will be out of action for a month.

> Announcement from the *Sporting Life* of 18 April 1977, open to various interpretations none of which seemed to be good news for Mrs Higgins

As a general rule we cannot have people going into the winners' enclosure and biting the jockeys' arses.

> Cartmel Clerk of the Course MAJOR TIM RILEY after an odd incident during a 1987 meeting at which jockey Phil Tuck had ridden a double and waitress Chrissie Kent showed her appreciation by nipping at his backside. Not the usual definition of a bum tip.

Bets on who will get stopped as they come through customs will not be taken. Nor will Corals accept wagers on whose bag will appear on the luggage carousel first, how many times the pilot will apologise for the 'short delay' nor who can empty the drinks trolley on a 50-minute flight to Paris.

> PAUL HAYWARD on the opening of a betting shop at Gatwick Airport *Daily Telegraph* 6 April 1994

Decided not to get married in 1981.

> Listed as 'Highlight of Career' by jump jockey BILLY NORRIS in the 1990 *Directory of the Turf*

I still think I lost – but I'm gonna take the money anyway.

> US trainer GARY JONES in May 1992 after one of his horses had been awarded a photo-finish verdict

I wouldn't have backed it had I known the true price.

> Philosophical comment from anonymous 'away' punter who, in July 1992, took 9/2 at Newmarket, about a horse which won at Pontefract, returning 100/1

I obviously feel let down to some extent.

> Jockey MICHAEL HILLS who, in July 1990, had just been sacked by his trainer/father Barry Hills

These two horses have met five times this season, and I think they've beaten each other on each occasion.

> JIMMY LINDLEY *Colemanballs 3* Andre Deutsch, 1986

. . . and there's the unmistakable figure of Joe Mercer . . . or is it Lester Piggott?

> BROUGH SCOTT *Colemanballs* Andre Deutsch, 1982

That's the magic of television – I've just heard over the headphones that Noalto was third.

> DAVID COLEMAN *Colemanballs* Andre Deutsch, 1982

That's what happened

I've never heard of anyone forgetting to weigh in after a walkover before, but that's what happened.

> Racecourse official at Blankney point-to-point where jockey Ciran O'Neill had just failed to win a one-horse race by omitting to weigh in *The Sun* 26 April 1994

He was yelling and cussing at me and telling me I had ridden a bad race. When he took his hands out of his pockets I just swung at him with my left hand.

> US jockey ALEX SOLIS speaking in December 1992 having just broken the nose of a Santa Anita racegoer

I came here 40-odd years ago and it was a lovely town then. But it's full of shit now. Horseshit, dogshit, every kind of shit. It's become the drug capital of Britain, and the lads these days are not a patch on the old ones. The horses have got more brains than most of them.

> JOE, the Newmarket cabbie, reported by Gary Nutting of the *Sporting Life* who was in Newmarket to interview Henry Cecil *Sporting Life* 23 March 1994

A broken-down old racehorse can go for five hundred or less at our less prestigious horse sales. In the meat markets of Belgium it will fetch around a thousand. Draw your own conclusions.

> PAUL HAIGH of the *Racing Post* confronting one of the 'mysterious questions', 15 January 1994

It was Graham Taylor's last good decision not to trouble himself with my signature on a contract.

> Trainer CHARLIE BROOKS, rejected by Watford as a potential goalkeeper when Taylor was their manager

Horseracing is worse. At least there aren't any squeaky voiced, shrimp-sized jockeys involved. You don't need binoculars. The races are finished in a few seconds, so there's no hanging around, glancing at your watch as the nags round the Canal Turn – again.

> ROBERT LEEDHAM, defending greyhound racing by comparing it with horseracing which, clearly, is not one of the loves of his life *The Guardian* 30 May 1994

Channel 4 Racing From Swindon.

> *Daily Telegraph* TV guide, 4 December 1993

I was referred to as 'the veteran Banbury handler'. That conjures up a picture for me of a dirty old man hanging around a street corner.

> 68-year-old trainer JOHN WEBBER *The Independent* 3 December 1993

We will regard any answer to the competition as correct and if anyone sends in the real correct answer that will also be right.

> A LADBROKE SPOKESMAN quoted in the *Daily Telegraph* City Diary, 3 December 1993, having been informed that the three offered answers to the bookies' 1994 Diary competition were all wrong

Would you like to speak to the horse?

> MARK PITMAN, overheard by racegoer John Morris in Bangor, answering queries from his mobile phone caller about the performance of fourth-placed Black Opal, 1 December 1993

Rescue me

Please come and rescue me, I'm stuck in the commentary box.

> Plaintive plea by RALEIGH GILBERT, broadcast over tannoy at Edinburgh in November 1993, 15 minutes after the last race. Wonder if he's still there.

I can honestly say it's a pain in the arse.

> Injured jockey RICHARD FOX on the pin in his damaged leg which had drifted out of position *Racing Post* 31 December 1993

Racing is the best fun you can have with your clothes on.

> Retiring jockey ANDY ORKNEY, 30 December 1993

I can assure you not even my mother had a penny on the horse.

> Red-faced *Times* racing correspondent RICHARD EVANS after his own Northern Saddler had won at 6/1 at Warwick – beating Evans' own Nap in the process *Sporting Life* 31 December 1993

It appears that within half a mile of the Jockey Club's HQ at Portman Square any man wishing to be hit with a whip with the same intensity as Adrian Maguire hit Barton Bank would have to pay £40 for the privilege.

> Letter from C. WILLIAMS to the *Racing Post* 4 January 1993, discussing the whip controversy

It will be the only show in town where you can follow up a good evening out by losing your shirt the next day.

> Writer KEITH WATERHOUSE on the scheme to insert a daily tip into the script of his 'Jeffrey Bernard is Unwell' at the Olympia Theatre, Dublin *The Times* 4 January 1993

I've just sent off for a 3D jigsaw. Should give me hours of fun.

> HENRY CECIL *Sporting Life* 23 March 1993

It's a bet I've had running with a mate for years. I've got to appear in front of the cameras to collect.

> Grimsby racegoer MICK ENRIGHT explaining why he is to be spotted on TV at every Cheltenham Festival, standing next to, behind or alongside jockeys and trainers as they are interviewed *Racing Post* 26 March 1994

I do believe horses are affected by a full moon, just like people are.

> Interesting observation by New York trainer CARL J. DOMINO – if he ever runs a horse called Werewolf, watch out!

That's the way I remember it.

> Bald-headed trainer CHARLIE 'Bald Eagle' WHITTINGHAM explaining why he listed his hair colour as brown when applying for his New York training credentials

Desert Orchid and I have a lot in common. We are both greys; vast sums of money are riding on our performance; the Opposition hopes we will fall at the first fence; and we are both carrying too much weight.

> Aware that an opinion poll had reported that Dessie was better known than the Chancellor of the Exchequer, NORMAN LAMONT produced these comments prior to the 1991 Budget. Which of them, though, will be the longer and more affectionately remembered?

Comfortable is having a horse in your own stable; rich is having a horse in the Derby.

> 'Journolists' in *You* magazine, 17 April 1994

The Queen Mother reads my books, you know, and I'd hate her to read them from my pen. I don't like writing about sex. Everyone knows I write about things that have happened to me or that I've been closely connected with. So I would hate people to think I was writing vivid sex scenes that I'd experienced.

It's also probably correct to say that I don't know enough about sex to write about it more than I do.

> In September 1993 racing thriller writer and former jockey DICK FRANCIS explained to Corinna Honan of the *Daily Mail* just why his bestsellers feature few sex scenes

I wouldn't even bring God down here.

> French trainer CARLOS LAFFON-PARLIAS whose hot favourite was left out of a race in San Sebastian after the stalls handler failed to install him

She's like Linford Christie – without the lunch-box.

FRANKIE DETTORI on Lochsong

There are no recorded members of an equine mile-high club.

GRAHAM ROCK discussing airborne arrangements for shipping British horses to the 1993 Breeders' Cup.

How did the runners at Taunton perform?

Heart attack victim CHESTER BARNES' first question upon recovering to his boss Martin Pipe

If Jesus Christ rode his flaming donkey like you just rode that horse, then he deserved to be crucified.

The late trainer FRED RIMELL to then amateur jockey Jim Old, reported by Marcus Armytage in *Daily Telegraph* 5 March 1994

Straight bananas

He only eats straight bananas.

CHESTER BARNES on one of the food foibles of his boss, Martin Pipe *The Champion Trainer's Story* Headline, 1992

I was determined to get round and the horse seemed game – he just needed a couple of attempts at each fence. By the end of the third (they started in the first) race we'd have done it. But I heard the commentator say, 'Come in, number 9, your time is up, we want to get the next race under way.'

Austrian rider HANS WALTL, carrying a mere 21lb overweight as he tried to complete the course at Braes of Derwent point-to-point on his own horse Simon. Simon refused twice at the second, again at the third, fourth and eighth and was lapped by all the other runners before the stewards called him in *Racing Post* 22 April 1994

I bowled him off his pads. It was a dreadful ball. He's never got out to one as bad as that before – or since.

JOSH GIFFORD who, incredibly, dismissed world record-scoring batsman Brian Lara of the West Indies in a 1991 charity game *Racing Post* 22 April 1994

Lara lofted a drive high into the air towards the boundary. The ball was coming at me too quickly to avoid making some attempt to catch it. So I held out my hands and, to my delight, when I opened my eyes the ball was lodged in my palms.

> A second racing personality with Lara's scalp to his credit – PETER SCUDAMORE, who caught him in another charity game, in 1992 *Racing Post* 22 April 1994

I put 'dead' by the wrong horse. I've apologised to everyone.

> Trainer RODNEY BAKER explaining how his Coochie, officially listed as being dead, managed to finish sixth in a hurdle race at Newton Abbot on 12 May 1994. I wonder if he apologised to the horse, too?

Time is only important if you are in jail.

> LUCA CUMANI's observation on the importance (or otherwise) of race-times, quoted by Monty Court *Sporting Life* 13 May 1994

To save Sheikh Mohammed a few quid on his entry fee.

> MICHAEL STOUTE on why he decided not to enter Hawker's News, Classic trial winner at Lingfield, in the Derby. A budgetary oversight which looked ill-advised as Hawker's News' form seemed to be rather more solid than some of the leading fancies for Epsom *Raceform Update* 14 May 1994

Betcha our girls do it better; Betcha our girls know how to help you enjoy your leisure; Betcha they give you a better service; Betcha our girls look different; Betcha you can get hold of them easily.

> Betcha Ladbrokes will not relish being reminded of this deeply sexist and non p.c. advertisement which they ran on the back page of a magazine called *Cover Girl* – not for sale to persons under 18 years of age – in its Volume One, Number One, among whose features was an 'Erotic Underwear Investigation'

E. Stack stated that he hadn't weighed himself for a month but thought he could do the weight.

> Report in the *Irish Field*'s Notice from the Calendar column after ten pound claimer Emmett Stack had weighed out at 8st 11lb at Down Royal to ride Tabu Lady who had been allocated 7st 8lb. They finished 11th of 14, inspiring a protest to the stewards by trainer William Rock, May 1994.

Yes, but I can't eat a whole one.

> Nomadic trainer ROD SIMPSON, asked whether he liked Wales, the location of his seventh and latest training centre, *Daily Telegraph* 23 May 1994

INDEX